THE MAP OF INNOVATION

THE MAP
of
INNOVATION

Creating
Something
Out of
Nothing

KEVIN O'CONNOR
WITH PAUL B. BROWN

CROWN
BUSINESS
NEW YORK

Published by Crown Business, New York, New York.
Member of the Crown Publishing Group, a division of Random House, Inc.
www.randomhouse.com

CROWN BUSINESS is a trademark and the Rising Sun colophon is a registered trademark of Random House, Inc.

Printed in the United States of America

Design by Robert Bull

Library of Congress Cataloging-in-Publication Data
O'Connor, Kevin (Kevin J.)
The map of innovation : creating something out of nothing / Kevin O'Connor.
1. Technological innovations–Management.   2. Creative ability in business.
3. Strategic planning.   4. Corporations–Growth.   5. DoubleClick, Inc.   I. Title.
HD45.O26   2003
658.4'063–dc21   2002155673

ISBN 1-4000-4831-1

10   9   8   7   6   5   4   3   2   1

First Edition

For Nancy, who always
supported my crazy ideas

CONTENTS

INTRODUCTION

HOW I INVENTED THE INTERNET

Al Gore did not invent the Internet. I did.

Let me tell you about it.

It was the late 1980s, and it was clear that the first company I helped start, ICC—which made it possible to link personal computers to mainframes—would suffer a long, lingering death.

There was nothing wrong with what our product did; it was just that the technology was in the process of changing. The migration to client-server computing was under way, and it was already clear that as personal computers became more powerful, the need to link to mainframes would steadily shrink—and so would our sales.

I was wondering what we could do about it when I stumbled across an idea. I asked myself: Why don't we develop a smarter terminal, one that would work with any computer system and take advantage of the power of the PC? What the world didn't need was fifty different "dumb" terminals, all hooking up to different systems. It needed one universal "smart" one. A system that you could communicate with directly, one that would let you link to anyone else who was part of it. This new terminal would support graphics, menus, scripting language, pictures, and more.

The idea, in short, was the World Wide Web.

As you know, despite my brilliant insight, I didn't invent the Web. But the experience of coming up with the concept taught me two important lessons:

1. Ideas are cheap. Once you have come up with one, you need to do something with it. (ICC executives, including myself, dismissed my idea for a universal terminal out of hand, because our company was trying to expand beyond terminals, not get deeper into them.)

2. If you really are going to do anything with your ideas—either inside an organization, or by starting one of your own—you need a process. You need a way to find the best idea you can; then, more important, you need the most efficient way to bring that idea to market by developing the best strategy, raising the money, and hiring the right people.

Through twenty years of trial and error, I think I have figured out a way to create something out of the nothing: creating new ideas and turning them into successful products in the market.

I have helped build three successful companies—ICC, which hooked the personal computers to mainframes; Internet Security Systems (ISS), now the leading Internet security firm; and DoubleClick, which allows companies to target their ads on the Internet effectively—using the processes I've developed. I am convinced these companies thrived in part because of the concepts I would like to share with you in the pages ahead.

While my background is in technology, these principles apply anywhere to any company, whether it is a technology-based start-up or a Fortune 500 retailer. In fact, I am using them today to help start two retail companies: one that hopes to be the category killer in action sports, and one that will change the way you rent movies.

You don't have to start a company to put these ideas to work. They are effective inside established organizations. I've used this process repeatedly both to conceive and extend product lines within the three companies I helped create.

You can, too. Who knows, maybe you'll come up with the idea that will become the next Internet. Just make sure you do something with it. The next few chapters will tell you how.

Santa Barbara, California
Spring 2003

THE MAP
of
INNOVATION

CHAPTER

ARE YOU SURE YOU WANT TO DO THIS?

Of course I know what I'm doing! What could possibly go wrong?
—RALPH KRAMDEN in almost every episode of *The Honeymooners*

If you knew the odds against creating a successful innovation, you'd never pursue it. If you are trying to extend an existing product line, you have a reasonable chance of success. But if you are trying to create something new, it is a totally different story.

Out of every hundred ideas, only one can be considered a good idea, an idea that has a chance of becoming a reality, whether you are starting from scratch or working inside an established organization.

Out of every hundred good ideas, only one is worthy of pursuit, of building a new company or division around.

Of those hundred start-ups, perhaps only one will be considered successful.

So, your odds of hitting a grand-slam home run are 1:100 × 1:100 × 1:100, or only 1/1,000,000. When the odds are literally a million to one, why even step to the plate?

And if you do step to the plate and try to get under way, you are bound to get depressed. The beginning stage of invention is the worst . . . and best of times.

Even as I write this I find myself in the start-up stage. I am always trying to start a new company. And now that I have the extreme sporting goods superstore and the consumer electronics product that I mentioned in the introduction well on the way to market, I want to do it all again. But I have no idea what idea I will pursue, and while I'm trying to figure it out, I know that the odds are stacked incredibly high against another success.

While I wait, I worry.

- What happens if I can't create a good idea?
- Or raise the money?
- Or hire great people?
- Suppose ten other people are already working on the same concept and beat us to market?

I'm starting to sweat just thinking about it.

But on the flip side, the beginning stage is also the most exciting. You can go in any direction. Maybe you'll become the greatest inventor since Thomas Edison or more powerful than Bill Gates (unlikely, but still . . .). Perhaps you'll create a company or even an entire industry that revolutionizes the world. Man, the beginning is an exciting time.

I guess that's why I keep doing it. I've helped create dozens of products and three separate companies, and I've invested in over a dozen early-stage companies. ICC was our first start-up; it helped pioneer the PC software industry by, among other things, making it possible for personal computers to connect to corporate mainframes. Sounds pretty boring now, but twenty years ago, it was voodoo!

ISS, with revenues over $200 million, is a leader in the security software space, serving more than nine thousand corporate clients worldwide, including forty-nine of the Fortune 50, ten of the world's largest telecommunications companies, and major agencies and departments within United States local, state, and federal governments.

And then there is DoubleClick, which people tend to lump in with eBay and Amazon when they talk about successful Internet survivors. DoubleClick is the leading provider of tools for advertisers, direct marketers, and Web publishers to plan, execute, and analyze their marketing programs. To oversimplify, our online advertising, e-mail marketing, and database marketing solutions help clients yield the highest return on their marketing dollar and also helps them measure performance within and across channels. We now employ more than fifteen hundred people in twenty countries.

Today I spend most of my time helping to start other new companies. Dave Strohm, a general partner at Greylock (a venture capital firm that helped fund both ISS and DoubleClick), described me awhile back as "a serial entrepreneur." I never pictured myself that way, but when I thought about it, I realized that, as usual, my friend was right.

Back in 1983, when I cofounded ICC, I had barely heard of the word "entrepreneur." Not only did I not know any entrepreneurs, I didn't know how to spell the word. (I think I got it right in the last sentence. I still have to spell-check it to make sure.)

> **Whether you are trying to create something new or innovate within an existing company, the steps are the same—and there is a process that will allow you to do it faster, cheaper, and better.**

A lot has changed in the past two decades, and I now talk to a lot of people who are thinking about starting companies or who have just started companies. In addition, I frequently meet people who want to become "intrapreneurs" (an ugly buzzword for an interesting process) and create new products and/or implement ideas inside the established companies for which they work.

Over the past few years, as I talked to these people and we traded stories about what we have done and hope to do, many of them told me I should write a book. As DoubleClick got more and more press, publishers got the same idea. I started receiving phone calls from editors who would ask me to write something about the "secrets" of starting a (technology) business.

I was always flattered, but I always said the same thing: I didn't have time. I was then CEO of DoubleClick, and I told them I needed to focus on running the business. (What I didn't tell them is that I knew writing a book is a horrible return on investment.)

Well, two years ago I handed over my CEO duties to Kevin Ryan, and while I'm still chairman of DoubleClick, I have a little more time on my hands.

WHY YOU SHOULD KEEP READING

I'm writing this book because there's been so little good stuff written about innovation and how you bring an innovation to market. I've found that most of the books out there simply talk about the importance of innovation, but not about how to do it. Or they tend to focus on ways you can increase your creativity–some of the stuff by Roger von Oech, such as *A Whack on the Side of the Head,* is good–but nobody, including von Oech, tells you either how to be creative systematically or how to bring your ideas to market.

Getting my process down on paper is why I wanted to write this book. In doing so, maybe in some small way, I can accelerate the innovation curve and we'll all live a little bit better. This process will help you avoid the numerous mistakes I made along the way (I will recount them in detail, so you know exactly what not to do). I know it can help you, because the process I describe here is the approach I followed in creating three separate successful companies and dozens of products.

As counterintuitive as it sounds, I think you can innovate methodically. You can force innovation. There is a process you can follow to improve both the number and the quality of ideas you can come up with.

I know this is true, because it is exactly what I have done in creating dozens of successful products. I've been a student of innovation for twenty years, and because I was never in a position to let the proverbial lightning strike me–I have too many obligations to wait for that, and even if I didn't, I don't have the kind of temperament that would allow me to wait for things to come to me–I needed to figure out a way to force innovation. It's that process of forcing innovation that you will learn about here, a process that I developed by trial and error over two decades and that has been refined and proven over time in a number of different industries.

> I only wish Thomas Edison had better documented his serial approach to innovation. I've always loved and agreed with his famous quote "innovation is 1 percent inspiration and 99 percent perspiration," which reinforces my belief that innovation can be forced. Edison would find a problem and work his ass off finding the best solution. That's what we're going to try to do here.

What's in it for you? This isn't a get-rich-quick book. If you are looking for that, put it down now and go buy some lottery tickets. The only people who get rich from those kinds of books are the people who write them, from consulting and speaking fees. I always strive to create companies and products that solve real problems, generate profits, and stand the test of time. I love technology and innovation, and I'm fortunate that I now get paid for what was once only a hobby: creating new ideas.

This book is targeted toward anyone who wants to innovate by:

- Creating something new from scratch–developing new products or services, or making existing processes more efficient within an existing organization. (I believe there are a lot of commonalties between a successful innovation within a company and a stand-alone innovation. In both cases, you have to create the idea; put together the strategy; get money; recruit the right people; and bring what you have to market, even if that market is internal. As you will see, the process you use is nearly identical.)

- Making something better. Organizations either innovate or die (to be replaced by firms that have figured out how to improve a product or service or solve a need).

In short, this book is designed for those people who share the passion and entrepreneurial urge to come up with a new idea and do something about it once they do either by starting a new company or improving an established one.

BATTING PRACTICE

So why should you listen to me?

I'm not a Ph.D. I don't even have an MBA. (I'm University of Michigan class of '83, bachelor of science in electrical engineering.) I'm not a consultant. And there are plenty of examples of people who have been far more successful entrepreneurs such as Thomas Edison and Bill Gates, two people I have tried to learn from.

Thomas Edison was one of the few people to create multiple inventions that not only spawned multiple industries but also radically changed our world: the incandescent lightbulb, the phonograph, and the motion-picture camera are three quick examples. Edison didn't chase "cool" technology; he focused on solving societal problems.

I think the best lesson I learned from watching Bill Gates is what I call "incremental innovation." Microsoft seems to believe that there is no way to truly learn about a market unless you are in it, and the best way to get into a market is to release a product. Their first version of a product is rarely the best, but through hard work and incremental innovation, they end up dominating many of their markets. Which of course leads to other problems . . . but that's not important here.

I've always tried to learn as much as I can from reading about innovators like Edison and Gates. Yet in all my reading, I couldn't find a common denominator among the best innovators, and that frustrated me. The biographies are more about what they did than how they did it. I wanted to find an approach that was reproducible. Of course, no approach can guarantee success, but I thought there had to be ways to increase your chances.

My metaphor for this is baseball. (I don't particularly like the sport, but the images work.) Let's say your goal is to get a hit off a Major League pitcher and you are a so-so athlete. What would you do?

Well, you might go up to the plate and give it your best shot. You could swing from the heels three times, and who knows? You might actually hit the ball, it might go fair, and you could get a hit.

But while it might happen, I think everyone would admit that the chances are pretty slim.

If you wanted to improve your odds, you'd probably focus on the fundamentals of hitting. You'd first learn how to swing the bat properly. You might start going to a batting cage, then work your way up to having good amateur pitchers throw to you. You'd study the pitcher you were about to face to figure out how he threw and to get an idea about what worked against him in the past.

Would all this guarantee success? Of course not. But if you focused on the *fundamentals,* it would improve your chances dramatically.

That is exactly what this book is about: improving your chances for success. You could go off and wildly try to create something new, and you might very well be successful. But the more you can develop a systematic plan that can improve your skills—and steer you away from problems—the better chance of success you will have, whether you are working inside an established company or starting something on your own.

So think of this book as a form of batting practice. It will let you focus on the fundamentals, the things you will need to do successfully. There is nothing more important when starting a company than to focus your full attention on the core fundamentals that will either make or break you. Too often people focus on things that simply don't matter, or they waste their time trying to find answers to questions that can't be answered. In every start-up or attempt to innovate within an existing organization, these are the fundamental issues that deserve your full attention:

1. Creating a large number of viable ideas
2. Picking the right idea to pursue
3. Creating a highly focused strategy to bring the idea to market
4. Getting the money to fund the strategy
5. Hiring great people to implement the strategy

And that's pretty much it. Everything else you do outside these five areas might prove to be a total waste of time. If you get the five things right, you improve your chances of success dramatically. If you get one of the five things wrong, you're not going to have much fun, because your new idea will fail, and that is no fun at all. You need to do all five things well.

Based on my own experiences and what I have learned from others, I have developed and refined innovation techniques over the past twenty years. These techniques work. That's the only conclusion I come to when I look back to find commonalities among the companies I helped to create, companies that now employ thousands of people and have generated many billions in shareholder value. While you can get lucky once, luck can't be the only explanation for my helping to create three successful companies and dozens of successful products.

I started down the innovation road a long time ago. One of the chores I had while I was growing up was taking out the trash. Every night I'd take out the garbage, and every night this huge raccoon would come behind our house, flip over the garbage can, and strew the garbage everywhere. Of course, I had to clean it up.

After trying lots of different ways to keep the garbage can from tipping over—none of which worked—I came to the conclusion that either I had to kill the raccoon or scare him off. You had to see this raccoon to appreciate the problem. They grow them big in Michigan. This animal was gigantic.

I love animals, so killing the world's largest raccoon wasn't an option. But something I had learned earlier was.

A few months before, I had accidentally discovered, as part of a different experiment, that if you touch a battery to the input leads of a television transformer, you generate thousands of volts of electricity that will hurl you across the room.

Armed with this painfully acquired knowledge of electricity, I rigged a trap involving a much smaller source of electricity and smeared it with peanut butter. I did that for two reasons. Peanut butter is moist, so it's a great conductor of electricity, and—equally important—raccoons love peanut butter. (To be honest, I think this raccoon would have eaten anything I put out.) When the raccoon stepped on the trap to lick the peanut butter, it would touch the leads to the battery and receive a shock.

I set out the trap that night, and we never had a raccoon problem again. (Before you write to People for the Ethical Treatment of Animals, let me tell you the raccoon didn't die. He was just scared off. At last sighting, he was foraging a couple of streets over, where I am sure he found the garbage more to his liking.)

I continued my inventions after college. Right out of school in 1983, I cofounded ICC, the software company I mentioned earlier, with Bill Miller and Mike Schier. During my next nine years there, as vice president of research, I created and brought to market more than twenty products, mostly along the lines of terminal emulation products that would tie PCs into Burroughs and Sperry mainframes. We also developed file transfer software and many other related ideas. We grew ICC to about $35 million in revenue by 1992, then sold it to Digital Communications Associates (DCA), where I eventually became chief technology officer.

In January 1995, DCA merged with Attachmate. My new boss told me innovation wasn't important, so I left to pursue the Internet, then a relatively unknown area. I was looking to start a company and searching for ideas. I soon met a twenty-year-old college dropout named Chris

Klaus who had created a unique security software product that could search out, find, and recommend potential fixes to computer network security problems.

I invested $50,000 and worked more or less full-time for the next four or five months writing the business plan, recruiting people, selling, and raising money, using many of the principles that I will outline in detail in this book. Today ISS is a public company with more than a thousand employees who offer companies of all sizes a way to detect, prevent, and respond to ever-changing Internet threats across networks, systems, and desktops.

I had a great time at ISS (I remain on their board), but I really wanted to start something on my own from scratch. I was convinced the World Wide Web was the place to be (in the next chapter, I'll explain the thinking that led me to that conclusion), so I teamed up with Dwight Merriman, who, like me, had gone from ICC to DCA. We came up with more than a hundred Internet ideas. To come up with potential businesses, we used the Brainstorming Prioritization Technique (BPT), which I will talk about in the next chapter.

As we thought of what we might do, our goal was simple: to create a huge Internet company. We didn't have any other preconceptions. Our ideas ranged from a site that would rate the quality of products on all other sites to a search engine that would locate the websites catering to your preferences in porn. (As I said, we didn't limit our thinking going in.)

One of the ideas we came up with—delivering extremely targeted advertising on the Web—became the foundation for DoubleClick, the company we founded in September 1995.

With DoubleClick, as with the other companies and products I helped to build, I followed the same general outline I'll present in this book. I believe that this approach, which has worked for me, will work for you. It should greatly increase your probability for creating a successful venture.

**This book won't guarantee that you will succeed,
but it should increase your chances.**

I worded that last sentence carefully. I know that what I am advocating will increase your chances of accomplishing your goals, but I am not guaranteeing success. No one can. As I mentioned at the very beginning, if you really considered what is required to innovate successfully, you'd have to wonder why anyone would try to innovate at all.

WHY WOULD ANYONE TRY ANYTHING NEW?

If you are looking for a secure career choice, innovating within an established firm or founding a new company is definitely not the place to start. The odds are just too long. If you want proof of how hard it is, you don't have to look any further than me. Even though I have figured out ways to increase my chances of success, I have had a number of misses. ("Misses" is a very polite word for losing all your investment.)

Here are some of my failures:

- A directory for professionals, similar to the *Physicians' Desk Reference* for medical doctors, went bust.
- A college note-taking service went under when they couldn't raise money in early 2000 after the public markets shut down.
- OpenMind, a revolutionary new groupware product, fizzled in the marketplace.
- I missed a huge opportunity with a remote LAN node (RLN) that I invented. RLN essentially allowed a PC to dial in to any local area network and act as if it were locally connected. (This is something we take for granted today.) We created the product when I was at ICC and never fully went after the market, missing a huge opportunity.

I feel marginally better about these misses when I consider that other innovators—people far, far more talented and smarter than I—experienced lots of failures as well. For example, Thomas Edison refused to patent his motion-picture inventions in the United States because he thought the fifty-dollar fee excessive. He patented them only in Britain: imagine the lost revenue! Albert Einstein never achieved his Unified Field Theory. The list goes on.

As you can see, there is no magic formula that will guarantee your chances every time at bat, even if you follow the ideas we are going to talk about here. But hey, even the most successful baseball players get a hit only one out of three times.

I'd love to be able to tell you the ten easy steps to innovation success, but they don't exist—and if you ever find a book making that promise, don't buy it. Success is a game of probabilities. By focusing on the key elements required to innovate successfully, we can hopefully increase your chances.

And that is what you have to do, try to increase your probabilities, instead of hoping for the best. Luck is great anytime you can get it, but the idea that you will be able to create a successful business randomly is as probable as winning the lottery (or, to go back to our previous metaphor, as probable as hitting a Randy Johnson fastball without any serious preparation).

If you apply this system, it's just like taking a lot of batting practice—your odds will go up.

In the next six chapters, I'll go through all the steps for creating something out of nothing. Though I won't spend a lot of time on it, I'll also show you how many of these techniques can be used to solve all sorts of business or even personal problems. The approach will work on any problem that requires an innovative solution.

While not everyone who applies these principles will be successful—in fact, few of you will—I'd love to hear about both your successes and failures. Please e-mail me at koconnor@kojjee.com.

IT'S ALL ABOUT TIMING AND APPROACH

I believe there are three key factors that determine if someone will innovate successfully:

1. Genetics; that is, you were born with a willingness to put ideas into action
2. Timing
3. Approach

This book focuses on timing and approach, because I don't think there's any way to change your genetics. The other two factors can help you enormously, but they cannot completely compensate for an internal drive to create. That is something I learned early on.

I had a dream when I was fifteen to win an Olympic gold medal in wrestling. I worked my ass off in high school to become a great wrestler. I lifted weights. I ran. I practiced long hours. The result? I turned out to be a good high school wrestler. But there would be no gold medal for me in the Olympics.

At the same time, there were others (you know who you are) who did half of what I did but went on to greatness in wrestling or some other sport. I didn't have the genes to be a great wrestler. (Obviously, it was all my parents' fault.)

But I think I was born an inventor. From my earliest memories, I was ripping apart and building things, and I have always looked for ways of doing things faster and better. For me, inventing is a hobby. I can't believe I get paid for it.

Do you have to be a natural inventor to be an entrepreneur or someone who can innovate effectively? I don't think so. Even though I never won the gold in wrestling, I still had a respectable career, and I was certainly far ahead of people with similar genetics who didn't work as hard. However, if you do have the natural ability, it raises the probability that you'll be successful. Still, everyone can improve.

As for timing, I firmly believe that big trends create big opportunities. When I look back on my own successes, I see that they all evolved around the three biggest tech trends over the past twenty years: personal computers, computer networks, and the Internet. (How you can spot trends of this size is part of what we will talk about in the next chapter.) Timing is certainly important. You want to have the best solutions to a problem—first, if at all possible. Life is much easier if you are first with the best solution. We'll talk throughout about how you can improve your timing.

As for approach, that's the focus of the rest of the book.

HOW THE BOOK WILL LAY OUT

A lot of people think that coming up with an idea is the key when it comes to innovation. It's not. The idea is important. But ideas are cheap. You have to come up with a lot of ideas and then pick the right one, the one you will focus on exclusively. The problem with good ideas is that you can come up with any number of them and get pulled in all directions. You need to concentrate. That is what the next chapter is about: How you can winnow down all your ideas to focus on the one that offers the greatest chance of success.

But you just don't need to have a lot of ideas to choose from to be successful. With every important decision, you want to have many options. The more options, the better the probability that you are picking the best alternative. The next chapter deals with that as well.

Every successful business must solve a problem or fill a need. The word "need" is important. Customers, whether you are selling to consumers or business to business, will pay to have their *needs* met. They may or may not buy the things they *want*. So, in the first version of your product, you must concentrate on customer needs. Don't try to satisfy their wants until the second or third version of your product. We will go into all of this is in detail in chapter 2.

Technology is increasingly becoming the critical component for delivering the best products and services at the lowest cost. When you apply the best technology to the biggest problems, you have the largest chance of success. (Your new idea doesn't have to have a huge technology component, but you will have more ideas to choose from if it does.) So creating products that satisfy customer needs–using technology to leverage that product whenever possible–is your starting point. With an idea firmly in place, and your vision locked in on what you are and, more important, are not going to do, it is time to implement your idea. That involves strategy (the subject of chapter 4). Strategy is everything you need to do to bring your idea to market and be successful. Usually, there are only these few things you really need to do, so the more resources and time you can focus on these few things, the greater your probability of success. In this chapter I will practice what I preach and concentrate on only the tasks you need to do, such as positioning your idea correctly; pricing it right; selling it well; and promoting it effectively. As you will see, your business plan is your strategy document.

Strategy in place, there are a lot of other things you *could* do, but there are two more things that you *must* do: determine how to get your necessary funding, and find the right people to hire to make your innovation a reality. These are the subjects of chapters 5 and 6.

My thoughts on money are pretty simple: raise three times more than you think you could ever possibly need, and do it at a time when you don't need it. Of course, that's a lot easier said then done as I sit here trying to help two consumer-product companies raise money during a terrible recession. We will talk about the progression you should follow in raising money, how you start by putting just about everything you own at risk, and going from there. We'll go through it step by step.

Hiring people is another area where innovators–and everyone else–tend to make things more difficult than they need to be. The key is to hire smart "athletes." As you will see in chapter 6, I'm not literally talking about hiring the captain of the Stanford football team–although

I certainly would try to get him if I could—but you want people who are bright, understand the need for hard work and for teamwork, and don't quit until they win. We will discuss why this is the case and more important, how to find these people.

And that's about it. I think we all make business a lot more complicated than it has to be. The secret, if there is such a thing, is to concentrate exclusively on the things you need to do and ignore everything else.

You'll notice that I talk a lot about what *needs* to be done, and I think this is probably the most essential point of the book: There are only a few things that need to be done to create a successful company, so focus all resources on just these needs.

Now let's start talking about how you can do just that.

CHAPTER

BPT: BRAINSTORMING PRIORITIZATION TECHNIQUE

Though this be madness, there is method in it.
—POLONIUS, from *Hamlet*

Innovation is the least understood phenomenon in business. We all know innovation is the secret sauce to whatever business meal you want to make, but how do you make the sauce?

That question took on enormous importance for me at ICC after we successfully built our first product, Intercom, which made it easy to connect personal computers to corporate mainframes. In the aftermath of that success, my biggest fear as an inventor was that I would get (to mix my metaphors) writer's block. I was scared that I wouldn't be able to come up with any new product ideas. And if you're the vice president of research, the person responsible for finding the next big idea, writer's block can be career-limiting.

I didn't want ICC to be a one-hit wonder. I knew there had to be a way to force innovation. I knew that because there were examples of it happening all around me:

- People and companies come up with new things when they absolutely have to. "Necessity is the mother of all invention" is a cliché that seems always to be true whether you talk about war (the atomic bomb) or business. Just to pick one example at random, Lotus developed Lotus

Notes very quickly once it became clear that Microsoft would destroy its flagship product, Lotus 1-2-3.

- Some people (Henry Ford, Thomas Edison, Bill Gates) and some companies (3M, Procter & Gamble, Cisco Systems) are flat-out better than others when it comes to creating new ideas.

These examples convinced me there had to be a process I could map and then follow, one that would allow me to innovate more effectively as I set off to build more products and companies. I already knew what the starting point would be: need.

When I looked at what I considered to be great innovations and/or great companies, they all seemed to be addressing a basic need.

For example, as we all began traveling more, we needed better ways to communicate, so cell phones and e-mail were invented. And as the Web became more central to everyone's life, we didn't have ways to make sense of it all, so search engines like Yahoo! and Google were created.

The take-away message was clear to me: At the heart of every great product is an unfilled need. If you can come up with a solution that meets the need, you will have a possible winner. (And, as we will see in the next chapter, if you can make that solution technologically based, you can leverage that success by an amazing degree.)

Maybe you're thinking that I just stated a ridiculously obvious fact about innovation, that it is all based on needs. Sort of like telling you to breathe. To judge from my own experience, whether it's in sports, religion, or business, it is the obvious that is always overlooked! More new companies were created during the Internet craze than in any previous period, and most of them forgot about filling a need. Maybe the ability to smell a new product online was an interesting idea to some people (ismell.com), but it didn't satisfy a basic need. And yes, being able to order food staples—either for you or for Fido—online would be convenient, but a need? Apparently not.

> Before BPT, I'd sit around and wait for ideas to strike me in the head.
> I sat around a lot. I thank God that the Internet wasn't around and
> that the personal computer I owned didn't have the game of hearts,
> or I would have wasted a lot of time.

For now the question is how can you come up with as many options as possible for creating something new? That is what this chapter is all about.

WELCOME TO BPT

People (especially my wife, Nancy) always tell me I have a Type A personality. And it's true. I can't stand to be in line. I don't want to wait. I need answers now.

More than anything, I hate wasting time.

And it always seemed to me that strategic planning meetings, when we tried to figure out where the company should be going, were a major waste of time in trying to create a new product or service.

Over the past 20 years, I've been involved with dozens of strategic planning efforts, as part of the companies I have been associated with, and each time the process seemed to go exactly the same tedious way.

Early on, when someone decided that innovating was a big deal, we'd hire a consultant and hold an off-site meeting, or a series of meetings, to try to come up with strategic alternatives. This process was incredibly costly. Not only were lots of senior managers devoting significant time to the process–time they could be spending generating sales and earnings for the company–but we also had the cost of the sessions themselves. We'd have to pay for a hotel or conference center located in some nice (read: expensive) place, food, the consultant, and all the follow-up materials. In one case, the total tab came to over $1 million, and the process took eight months.

More frustrating, from my point of view, was that we wasted an awful lot of time. We typically had 95 percent of the strategy done on the first day. By the time we completed the initial session, we knew what we needed to do. The remaining time—often months and months—was spent in useless meetings where we attempted to validate the ideas we had come up with. How big would the marketplace be? Who exactly would buy the product? What would our market share be in year one? In year five? It went on and on.

You can imagine what a pain in the ass I was during those follow-up meetings. I couldn't understand why we weren't doing what it seemed we all knew we had to do.

We needed to get off the pot.

Being naturally impatient, I was desperate to find a way to shrink the entire process of idea generation and strategy to one day. My intuition told me that if you put a bunch of smart people in a room, most of the answers were bound to be in that room. You just needed:

1. A way to draw out all possible answers
2. A way to narrow the many possible answers to only a few of the best
3. A way to build consensus

Not only would following this three-step approach save time, it would give me a process to use each time I wanted to create something new. It would eliminate my "writer's block" worry.

More time. Less worry. Life would be good!

So, I sat down and tried to figure out exactly what the process should look like.

Now, I didn't create this out of thin air. I tried to synthesize everything I had ever read about innovation—borrowing heavily from the way advertising and consulting firms do it—and everything I liked and disliked about the innovation efforts I had been involved with. Many people are familiar with this technique; the bigger issue is how it is applied to many of the innovation steps. The result led to what I call the Brainstorming Prioritization Technique (BPT). It's an awful name, I know, but it completely describes the process.

Here's how it works.

The first thing you have to do, whether you are trying to come up with a new idea or improve an existing product or service, is to make sure you have the right people in the room. If you are talking about a specific area—such as how to improve customer service—you certainly may want representatives from the customer-service department present. But having only those people in attendance would be a mistake. You should also include others who interact with or depend on customer service.

As an alternative or a supplement to the group you have assembled, you might want to invite a couple of really smart employees, people who seem to have the knack for creativity in any area.

The reason for having these additional people present is simple. The easiest way to get unconventional thinking is to invite people who don't even know what the conventions are. They may prove to be like the little girl who doesn't see the emperor's new clothes.

The point is that you need to have the right people in the room. By "right people," I mean those who know about the problem you're going to discuss, the ones who have the facts and are going to be affected by whatever decision you make. And you want to have present people who are really smart and innovative. Hopefully, everyone in the room will fall into both camps.

While you are figuring out who should be part of the BPT session, don't be afraid to invite the other half of customer service—i.e., customers or people you would like to be your customers. At DoubleClick, we've used BPT with customers to a great extent. We hold periodic off-the-record dinners during which we ask clients to give their view on two questions:

- What will the Internet look like in three to five years?
- What are the biggest obstacles keeping us from getting there?

From this we get a good sense of the problems facing our clients. A client's problem is an opportunity for us. Several of our products have evolved directly from the results of these meetings. For example, clients told us that as they expected to do more and more business over the Internet, they would need a good way of tracking all the activity on their site: who was visiting, what they were buying, how often they were returning. We designed products that allow them to know exactly what was going on.

BPT IN ACTION

Once I've selected the right people, I follow a pretty straightforward process that doesn't generally vary. It should be consistent for you as well. The size of your company and your ultimate goal don't matter, whether you want to create a new company or improve an existing idea.

Let's go through them now.

What you need: flip chart, markers, paper, pens, a comfortable room, three to ten participants, and a leader. Oh, and no cell phones.

The first part of this list is self-explanatory, but let's spend a minute on the size of the group and who should lead it.

Since you want to generate as many ideas as possible, you probably don't want to go through this exercise by yourself. Yes, you could do it alone and come up with a surprisingly large number of ideas if you let yourself concentrate, but you'll come with more ideas from the BPT process if you have a few people with you.

But don't have too many people. With more than ten participants, the process gets unwieldy. Groups over 10 become difficult to manage.

And there's another problem. Some people are too shy to talk if they are part of a big group. If you find yourself with more than ten people, break into two (or more) groups and run the process in parallel.

Who leads the group(s)? I like to have people who can make sure that everyone stays on track and keep up with what's going on. Their rank doesn't necessarily matter, but they need to have the confidence to stand up to the more senior execs who are part of the session.

There is nothing wrong with having the CEO—or whoever is the highest-ranking person in the room—lead the discussion. But if that's you, remember, you're there as a facilitator. You want to hear what everyone has to say. Coax out all the ideas from everyone. You can include your own thoughts during the brainstorming, but you don't want to stanch the flow of ideas, even inadvertently. Be careful when you chime in, and keep making it clear that you are there to help make sure the session runs smoothly and as just another participant, not as someone who knows *the* right answer.

Okay, with the housekeeping chores out of the way, it is on to the process itself. The first thing you need to do is define the problem. You want to answer: "What need are we trying to fill?" That can be a lot harder than it sounds. You must be specific.

While you could simply ask, "What do businesses and/or consumers need?" you could narrow it down substantially. You could, for example, focus on consumers purchasing products on the Internet. If you go that route, you might phrase the question like this: "What do consumers need when they buy products on the Internet?"

It's best to state the problem simply, but in terms that encompass the actual problem. Be careful not to reduce things too far. If you overly define the problem, you might end up focusing on the symptoms and not the actual problem. Let's go back to our earlier customer-service example to show you what I mean.

You might have a problem in customer support. Say the number of calls coming in is overwhelming you. You could assume that the problem is not having sufficient phone lines, or not having enough people to handle the calls. If you focus on the phone system, you'll miss the opportunity to fix the real problem, which is "Why are we getting so many phone calls?"

Before we move on, let me make three points.

First, some people think that the only goal of going through the BPT process is to create an idea that will change the world. It doesn't have to be. Not everyone wants to change (or rule) the world. Many entrepreneurs are happy to find innovations that solve a small but important problem. Besides, I like to think that all innovations tend to change the world in some way.

The second point is more troubling. A lot of people freeze right before beginning BPT. They desperately want to make sure they think of every possible idea. They worry about how they'll capture every option, and they constantly second-guess themselves during every point in the process by wondering, "What if this happens?" "What happens if that happens?" "What if . . ."

Their concern is understandable, and it is something I wrestle with every time I use BPT. You're never absolutely certain. You can't be. But here is the important point. With BPT, you are provided with many *options*, and the more options you have, the more likely you are to discover the best possible one. Worrying about whether you capture every choice is a waste of time. As I said before, you can never be absolutely sure.

My wrestling coach used to confront the what-ifs by saying, "You could get hit by a car crossing Outer Drive [the busy street our school was on]. Does that mean you're never going to cross the street?"

The BPT process is not about creating certainty. It's about increasing the probability that you will be successful by flushing out as many good ideas as possible. BPT is also like exercising your brain. When you train your brain to be creative, you'll naturally be more creative. The brain is an amazing computer, one that adapts and grows like a muscle if you exercise it. The more often you go through the BPT exercise, the more innovative you will become.

Certainty is impossible when you are dealing with innovation and the future. You can never achieve certainty. You can, however, increase your odds of being right, and that is the goal behind the Brainstorming Prioritization Technique.

Third, BPT is a great way to solve almost any problem. Let's say your family members don't know what they want to do on vacation. You could brainstorm about what activities everyone wants to do while you are away from home (ski, sit on the beach, eat, sleep, sail, etc.), then narrow the list down to the most important activities for the group. Next, you could brainstorm on destinations that meet your needs. This builds consensus within the family, which is always a good thing to do, especially if there are kids involved.

People often asked me, "what are the secrets for creating a successful company?" I knew there weren't any "secrets," in fact they are all obvious. The only "secret" was to identify which things you *need* to do well in order to build a successful company or product.

I used BPT to figure out what I wanted to accomplish when I stepped down as CEO of DoubleClick. I also used it to write this book. Here's how.

One day I sat down and used BPT to build the outline of this book. I brainstormed about all the things you could do to build a company or product, then narrowed the list to the few things you *need* to do to build the product or company. Each of these needs (idea, technology or trend, strategy, money, and people) created the basis for a chapter.

We are not going to spend much more time on how BPT can be used outside the workplace. This is a business book, after all. But I wanted to make sure the thought that BPT can be used in nonbusiness settings didn't get lost along the way.

With all this in mind, spend ten to twenty minutes brainstorming all possible solutions to the problem. No discussion is allowed during brainstorming, and all ideas should be kept to three to five words. No suggestion is out of bounds. The leader should capture it, write it on the flip chart, and move on.

When the ideas stop coming, try to rephrase the problem (perhaps in the negative) to start the flow again. For example, if your goal is to figure out what you have to do to create the best Internet retail site, you would start off by asking, "What do people want to buy?" When the ideas start to dry up, you might ask, "What don't people want to buy on the Internet?" It could spur a whole new round of thoughts.

Remember: During the actual brainstorming, you don't want to discuss any ideas. There will be plenty of time for that later. You don't want discussion to stop the flow or get off on a tangent. The key to brainstorming is that one idea spawns another idea and then another. When ideas are flowing, people are more apt to throw out silly suggestions, and you'll find that sometimes those silly suggestions aren't so silly—they are revolutionary. The "no discussion" rule also keeps the effect of strong personalities to a minimum. Those folks throw their ideas out there just like everyone else.

When the group has run out of steam—and that will probably happen within twenty minutes, although there is no right amount of time—give people the opportunity to clarify anything they've said. (If that triggers a couple more ideas, terrific.) This clarification period also gives people the chance to lobby (subtly) for the brilliance of an idea.

Once everyone is clear on exactly what the ideas are, the leader should number each one. As she does, the leader and the group should search for places where similar thoughts can be combined. There will be some overlap, usually 10 percent or so—look for places to simplify the list.

There's no typical brainstorming session. From my experience, you'll probably end up with anywhere from twenty to a hundred ideas.

For the sake of this discussion, say you end up with thirty-six distinct ideas once the overlap has been eliminated.

Out of thirty-six ideas, how do you find the big idea? You need a way to winnow down that list. Here's how to do it. Divide the total number of different ideas (in this case 36) by three. In our example, you end up with twelve. This is the number of votes everyone gets, one-third the number of ideas.

Since the ideas are already numbered, each person simply writes down the number of the ideas he wants to vote for.

There are three things to note about how the voting process works:

1. **People can put only one vote against an idea.** Even if you're convinced there's one perfect idea, you can't throw all of your twelve votes against it. You can vote for it only once.

2. **There is no sandbagging.** Say you know one idea that you like is going to win. You still have to vote for it. You can't save that vote and put it toward another idea.

3. **You don't have to cast all your votes.** Vote only for the ideas that you think have merit. If you have twelve votes but you like seven ideas, then vote for the seven you like. There is a maximum number of votes you can cast, but no minimum.

Give people a few minutes to decide how they want to vote. They should simply write the number of the idea they want to vote for on a piece of paper they hold on to. The leader then goes through the list, calling out the number of each idea one at a time. As the number is called, people raise their hands if they voted for the idea. Put the total votes next to the idea. After everyone has voted, tally up the scores. A few of the ideas probably will have received the most overwhelming number of votes.

Let's say you had ten people in the room who were voting for those eighteen ideas. The breakdown might look like this:

Idea	Votes Received
1	3
2	13
3	12
4	2
5	17
6	2
7	12
8	1
9	3
10	2
11	16
12	3
13	4
14	18
15	3
16	4
17	2
18	3

When the votes are in, look for the logical break points—which ideas got the plurality of votes. In this case, ideas 2, 3, 5, 7, 11, and 14 are the clear winners. That is fairly representative of how the process works. You are looking to end up with three to six ideas. These three to six top vote getters are the ones you keep, so look for the logical break in votes to determine the exact number.

In a few rare cases, you may not end up with an obvious consensus. The votes might be spread fairly equally across a number of ideas. In that case, the problem might lie in the way you asked the question initially, or in people not knowing exactly what they are supposed to do. If you have a situation like this, renumber the ideas that contain at least one vote, and spend some more time discussing each one of them. Then vote again. In the end, you need to reach a strong consensus on three to six ideas.

Once you do, you'll have your best ideas. Disregard everything else.

That last point is important. When you have identified the top vote-getters, there is no looking back. After the voting is over, people don't get a chance to lobby for their favorite(s) that didn't win. Those ideas are history, at least for now. You have separated the wheat from the chaff. You throw out chaff. It is time to move on to the next phase.

These three to six ideas are it. There is no looking back.

Of course, persuading people to let go of an idea that didn't get enough votes can be difficult. They often have a lot of themselves invested in their ideas, and they don't want to let them go, regardless of the voting.

Sometimes they don't have to. BPT is an iterative process, so you will be brainstorming the same question several times as you research the idea. There is often a chance for an old idea to resurface later, and the second or third time it does, it may garner enough votes to be considered. Occasionally, old ideas that didn't seem so good one day look brilliant later on as a market changes.

But that doesn't happen frequently. Then you have to explain to the person who feels her idea was slighted that the vote has been taken, and the group is going to research the ideas that have gotten the most votes and ignore everything else. You have to tell her it's like what they say about appeals to God. Everyone's prayer is answered, but sometimes the answer is no. When it comes to the creation of new ideas, everyone in the room is playing God (and sometimes saying no), and everyone in the group has to abide by the results.

At least for the time being. What frequently happens is that everyone leaves from a BPT session, and then hours, days, or months later, a new idea pops into your head. This isn't a problem; it's a great opportunity. During the next iteration of BPT, include these ideas to see if they make the cut. As I said before, BPT is brain exercise, and you are far more likely to have lightning strike as a result of going through the BPT process.

In the next chapter, you will see how the process led to the creation of DoubleClick. We followed the same road map we laid out here; indeed, it is the process I always follow in trying to create either a new product or a new company.

ADVANTAGES OF THIS SYSTEM

BPT is designed to get all the ideas on the table and quickly build a consensus as to which are the most promising. (Your research—something we'll talk about later—will determine the best one.)

As you have already figured out, BPT is a great way to eliminate a common problem of organizations of any size: people trading on their access to senior management to try to get their ideas adopted.

You'll recognize this situation: Joe comes up with an idea and is able, through his personality or a prior relationship, to convince the boss that he has the best idea. That may very well be the case. But the rest of the group feels no ownership to the idea, and maybe a few of us even dislike Joe, so we have no incentive to make his idea work.

> By the time you've figured out the one concept you're going to pursue, nobody remembers who initially came up with the idea that got the most votes, which helps remove personality conflicts and build consensus in the BPT process.

BPT eliminates this problem. If Joe's idea doesn't get enough votes—and remember, he had a chance to make his case during the clarification period after all the ideas were thrown on the table—then it isn't pursued. If Joe's idea does have merit, it should become evident with BPT. (We'll just have to find another reason not to like Joe.)

Do the results of BPT have to be followed straight down the line? Of course not. If the CEO or person responsible for the BPT's outcome likes an idea that doesn't get the most votes, he has the right—and, I would argue, the obligation—to place it among the ideas that will be researched. BPT doesn't have to be completely democratic, but the assumption of everyone in the room should be that it will be.

What I really like about the Brainstorming Prioritization Technique is that you get a lot of diverse options on the table very quickly, it *forces* people to prioritize, and it builds consensus. (If people can't accept the ideas that earn the most votes, they are free to leave the team and ultimately the organization if they disagree strongly enough. As we will discuss in chapter 6, where we talk about how you find and retain the best employees, people who work for an organization need to believe in what it is doing. And the best organizations focus relentlessly on the factors that will make them successful.)

No individual or organization can do fifty things well, and no individual or organization can effectively research fifty potential projects. But you can closely examine three to six—the ideas that got the most votes.

This isn't to say you can develop those three to six ideas, but you can research that many. After the research, you might realize you have two or three great ideas to pursue. Sometimes that's too bad, especially if you're starting a new company, since you often can pursue only one. But the fact is you have to focus, and that means coming up with what appears to be the best idea and leaving everything else behind.

As I said before, ad agencies, consultants, and other creative industries use similar techniques in their never-ending search for the next huge creative breakthrough. So I did not invent the idea. I have just refined these traditional approaches and applied it to creating business ideas and strategy as a means of forcing innovation.

Let me use a very simple real-life example to illustrate how BPT plays out inside an established organization.

A couple of years ago, DoubleClick was growing at an amazing rate.

(Every company should have such problems.) This was back when seemingly a million people a day were discovering the Internet, and advertisers were trying to reach all those people.

As the leading company helping marketers target their message on the Net, we were the logical place for advertisers of all kinds to turn for assistance. But we were growing so fast that we were struggling to discover the real issues inside the company.

This was an especially difficult problem for me. Few people want to tell the CEO what the company is doing wrong, and few CEOs like to hear it. To help me find out what was truly going on, we started a monthly luncheon program in which we would bring in around fifteen people from throughout the organization. As I told everyone who attended, the purpose of the lunches was to figure out how to increase employee morale and productivity. Period. No hidden agendas. No tangential issues. For these sessions, we weren't concerned with anything outside DoubleClick; we had a strictly internal focus.

To make sure I captured all the ideas, I followed the BPT process exactly as I've described it to you. I began by writing on a whiteboard: "How can we improve DoubleClick?"

The question got dozens of responses, ranging from "We need to spend more time on new employee training, so that a new hire can get up to speed faster" to "We need better controls on expenses, so that we can boost our bottom line."

When the idea flow ended, I'd posed the question in a few different ways to see if I could coax out any additional ideas. For example, I asked:

- If a truck hit me the moment I left this room (a real possibility in New York) and the board of directors named you CEO, what would be the first thing you'd do to improve conditions here?
- What part of your job really sucks? What procedure or process are you required to do that you find adds zero value to anyone or anything?

The first time I did this exercise, there were more than a hundred ideas about ways to improve the organization. I ran out of room on the whiteboard. After I got done writing down all the ideas, I stared at the list and got pretty depressed. It seemed like we weren't doing anything right.

After the brainstorming, the group voted to identify the three to six top issues. Based on the balloting, we initially decided to concentrate on additional training, cutting expenses, improving customer support, and communicating better. These were the four topics that got the most votes. I then went to the people who could implement the ideas we came up with (or who had the authority to kill the procedures that were hampering the organization), and we talked about how to make those ideas a reality.

Over time the number of ideas slowed down to around twenty or so each time we held a BPT session: proof that the system was working.

Many of our major internal programs came directly from these luncheons. For example, in a surprise suggestion that we control employee expenses better—employees usually want less control on expenses, not more—we created and enforced travel policies. We started an intranet so that we could communicate better company-wide, and we put a sales management system in place to better serve our customers. There is no doubt that BPT has improved our company and made innovation and improvements happen more quickly.

BPT CHECKLIST

1. Get the right people in the room.
2. Define the problem carefully.
3. Spend up to twenty minutes brainstorming, no discussion.
4. Explain and talk about the ideas until everyone is clear what they are.
5. Combine similar ideas.
6. Number the ideas.

7. Divide the total number of ideas by three. This is the number of votes each person gets.
8. Only one vote per idea.
9. Circle the top three to six ideas. Ignore everything and begin your research.

CHAPTER

3

TECHNOLOGY → NEED = SOLUTION

You can't always get what you want.
But if you try sometime, you just might find
You get what you need!
—The Rolling Stones

We make business too complicated. Here's an example. Recently, I was one of several guest speakers at a panel discussion. Another member of the panel started a lengthy discourse about Aristotle's influence on his business. I had to interrupt him to ask, "Are you speaking about Aristotle in the original Greek or in translation?"

The audience cheered. I didn't mean to embarrass the guy, but *Aristotle*? Geesh.

He was doing what all of us do. He was making business too complicated.

All business, no matter what business you are in, really boils down to answering three questions:

- Who are your customers?
- What are their needs?
- How can you solve those needs most efficiently?

Answering those three questions is what this chapter is all about.

> The basic theory is this: If you can apply the best technology to solve
> a basic need, you will have solved the problem most efficiently.

WHAT'S AHEAD

The three questions you have to answer are simple and direct. So is the
process for solving them.

- You use BPT to identify lots of consumer or business needs, which you
  then narrow down to a handful.
- You use BPT to identify all the possible technologies you might use,
  which you also narrow down to a handful.
- You use BPT to apply that handful of technologies to the handful of
  needs, and potential solutions pop out.

In this chapter, I will show you how you to create a chart that
matches customers' needs to existing and/or emerging technologies.

ONE QUICK CAVEAT

Before we start, let me make one large qualification about technology. I
do believe it will play a critical role in most future companies and ideas.
Technology can help provide the fastest, best, and cheapest solutions to a
wide variety of products. However, that isn't the case for every company.

Even as I write this, I'm involved in the early stages of a retail-action
sporting goods company. It will be the one place you'll need to go if
you're into extreme sports. This idea addresses a major consumer trend,
but one in which technology plays a minimal role.

If you find yourself pursuing an idea for which technology does not
play an important role in satisfying the customer's needs, then ignore
my upcoming technology discussion.

In your case, you may want to substitute trends for technology. Ask yourself what trends, be they demographic (Generation Xers coming to the fore), sociological (people retiring earlier), or economic (more and more businesses outsourcing) you can apply to needs.

However, if technology could play an important role—and I think in the vast majority of cases it will—and you ignore it, beware. The tech-based company will supplant you. Technology is more efficient than human beings, and it works for a heck of a lot less.

There is a reason we will put technology in the second half of this chapter. The process we outlined above works whether you apply needs to technologies or technologies to needs. But you will probably get a broader list of potential products and services if you begin with needs. Begin by asking what a consumer or business wants: That will give you more options than by starting with overly broad questions such as "How can we apply human genome research?"

So, let's spend the first part of the chapter on needs, then move on to the technology that can help satisfy those needs, remembering that in the rare case when technology isn't relevant, you will want to substitute "trends" for "technology."

PART I: NEEDS

A customer can be a business, a nonprofit, or the government, in addition to being a traditional consumer, but no matter who that customer is, if you aren't satisfying their need, you won't have a company.

How do you know what a customer needs? The answer all depends on what you are trying to do and where you are in the process of innovating. If you work inside an established company, you may already know what your existing customers need. Either the people you do business with have told you, or an opportunity has become clear as you have spoken with customers—and former customers. Sometimes, someone may ask you for something that isn't currently on the market. (Later, I'll give you an example of that happening to me.)

If you are starting from scratch, as we were with the process that eventually led to the creation of DoubleClick for example, you may not know what the need is. You have to find out. You come up with as many ideas as possible. That's where the Brainstorming Prioritization Technique (BPT) comes in.

Once you generate all those ideas and narrow them down to a manageable number, you ask customers if they would be willing to pay for what you've come up with. If they are, they have a need.

But our starting point in either case is an assumption that you have some level of knowledge about the area in which you think there is a customer need. You don't have to have a lot of knowledge. When we started DoubleClick, we didn't know any more about advertising than the typical businessperson. But you don't want to start completely from scratch. You don't have that kind of time. If you have to spend years learning the basics, don't do it. While you're spending all that time learning, someone will beat you to market. Pass on the idea. That's what a company I'm associated with did recently. It decided not to pursue what I know could be a huge business.

Here was the idea: Because so much business is done over the Internet, and because so much of that business involves contracts, we looked at developing a business around the idea of digital signatures—the ability to sign an electronic form over the Internet. It will eventually be big, as all of us do more and more business electronically, but it won't be an area we'll pursue.

We decided to pass for two very practical reasons. First, the market won't develop quickly. While it is inevitable that we will all sign contracts and documents electronically, not all of us will start doing it overnight. The idea of signing something important in ink is so ingrained that electronic forms will take a while to catch on, since they involve changing a basic habit as well as state and federal laws. ("Copy and paste your John Hancock here"?)

The second reason for not pursuing the idea was just as basic. We didn't have the necessary specialized technical background. We didn't know enough about digital signatures and the legal changes that will be required, and learning how to do it well would take too long. While we were learning, someone invariably would beat us to market and there are probably dozens of specialized companies already pursuing the idea. For both those reasons, we've discarded the idea.

The point is, it definitely helps to have some sort of knowledge or experience in the area you're going into. While it was true that we didn't know much about the media in general and the advertising industry in particular when we started DoubleClick, we did understand the technology (Web, browsers, database, commercial software) that would form the infrastructure for everything we hoped to do with the company. We had that by way of background. The fact that we didn't know the advertising business actually worked to our advantage, because we were too dumb to know what we weren't supposed to do (not always a great résumé point, but ideal for a start-up). To turn a cliché inside out, we were able to think outside the box because we didn't know where the box was. Thinking outside the box, however, has to have reasonable limits.

> Many of the world's greatest innovations came from people outside the existing market. Percy LeBaron Spencer, a physicist at Raytheon, invented the microwave oven after accidentally melting a candy bar in his pocket with microwaves during one of his research projects.

For example, for us to come up with something that involved an advanced technology such as gene therapy (or even digital signatures) wouldn't have made any sense. It would take years for us to gain the necessary background.

When I tell potential innovators that they must have some understanding of the market in which they are trying to solve a need, they nod and say, "Of course." Then they promptly go too far in the other direction. If their background is in commercial real estate, that's where they focus all their attention. They look within that narrow space. That might not be the best approach. You'd be surprised how much you know about areas outside your particular field of expertise. Certainly, a commercial real estate expert knows more than you and I do about building costs, contractors, and residential real estate, but he has even more knowledge than that.

A real estate expert, like all of us, uses certain tools in his line of work. He might try taking one of them—such as the multiple listing service (MLS), which displays every home for sale in a given area, not just the ones represented by an individual real estate office—and see if it can be applied elsewhere. Maybe the MLS approach could work for the selling of cars or boats.

Also like all of us, a real estate expert is a consumer. We can each come up with a list of things we would love to improve about our interactions with retailers. I am sure you could come up with three things right now that make your life harder than it needs to be when you are trying to buy something.

It's no different with your business. You work in a business, and that means you deal with expense reports; you interact with a sales department; you meet with customers. You know what works at work and what doesn't, so you can see needs that aren't being met.

In DoubleClick's case, even though we didn't know the ad industry inside and out, we'd been exposed to ads our whole lives; we knew advertisers want them to be not only memorable but effective; and we felt a service that could help them achieve this would satisfy one of their basic needs.

It is usually when you apply your expertise to a different but related area that innovation occurs.

So, don't limit yourself to places where you've spent most of your professional life. Think more broadly. For example, include what you do outside of work. If you love the outdoors and you know something about camping, biking, or kayaking, don't be afraid to look there. I recently went spear fishing and became frustrated when I couldn't load my prehistoric spear gun (which is currently state-of-the-art) fast enough to take a shot at a school of yellowtails who were laughing at me. I know I can invent a faster-loading spear gun.

But it's always dangerous to use yourself as an extension of the marketplace. Looking for opportunities that you feel passionately about is like a good-news/bad-news joke. Let's deal with the good news—why it's a great idea—first.

If you really like the area—the outdoors, commercial real estate, garage sales, whatever—that's a major plus. The more you love your idea, the more you believe in it, the more passionate you'll be. I think at the end of the day, it's much better to pursue an idea that you're passionate about than to pursue the best idea. Starting a company or innovating within a company takes a lot more than hard work. It requires total dedication. It requires you never to have any doubts. If you have doubts, don't do it. As Yoda said in *The Empire Strikes Back:* "Do or do not. There is no try."

You need to believe. To be blunt, the odds are good that your venture will not be successful, so it is better to be poor and happy (you gave it your best shot) than poor and sad (because the venture that failed was one you weren't all that passionate about in the first place).

For example, when Dwight Merriman and I were thinking of what Internet-based company we might start, we concluded that adult entertainment would be huge. We knew—and remember, this was in the mid-1990s—that pornography was going to be really big on the Internet. We were dead-on. But the idea wasn't something we were passionate about. (It also wasn't the sort of thing that would make Mom and Dad proud, let alone rush for their checkbook, and Mom and Dad were potential investors for whatever we chose to do.) So we decided not to pursue it, even though we knew it would be a big market.

So you need to be committed to your idea. Now for the bad news. Just because you're passionate about something doesn't mean that anyone else is going to be. That's why it's risky to delude yourself into thinking that you're the typical consumer. It may turn out that you are indeed Mr. or Ms. Everyperson. But don't go into the process think-ing that you are. There is a danger in starting a company around that premise alone. To use a ridiculous example to drive home the point: There is no call for designing a better subway system if most of your po-tential customers live in Nebraska, and improvements to milking ma-chines will find few takers in Manhattan. (And it's likely there's a very small market for fast-loading spear guns, which is why I probably won't develop one.)

Yet don't close yourself off to the possibility of coming across some-thing in your everyday life that could turn out to be a billion-dollar idea. Solutions to needs can come from anywhere.

Let me give you an example. I rent a lot of movies. I mean a lot. Like everyone else, the thing I hate about it is having to return the movie after watching it. In fact, the entire movie-rental business is built around a bad solution to a consumer need. The movie-rental compa-nies, like Blockbuster, make you go to the store to pick up the movie, and then they make you go back to the store to return it.

As a consumer, you don't want to return the movie. (You've seen it. You're done with it!) But that's where the industry makes its money. Sure, they're hoping you'll rent something else when you go back. But what they really hope is that you won't return the movie on time.

Here's why. Most people rent on the weekends—Friday, Saturday, and Sunday. That means the vast majority of inventory sits on the shelves unrented Monday through Thursday. If you rent a tape or DVD over the weekend and forget to return it until Tuesday or Wednesday, that's pure profit for the rental place. Your keeping the movie those extra couple of days is generating income for them, instead of having it sit unwatched on the store shelf.

I am convinced this economic model is also why video stores offer you a two-for-one discount during the week. They figure you'll be too busy to get both movies back on time on a weekday. (That reminds me, I have three overdue DVDs this very moment.)

The entire business is based on the consumer making mistakes. It's a flawed model. It's as if the car business were based on the automobile breaking down so the car companies could charge you for repairs. Net-Flix has done a great job of eliminating late fees, but it's sill inconvenient to rent and return the DVDs.

My firsthand experience with the flawed business model that is at the heart of the movie-rental business is what got me interested in all this in the first place. It ultimately motivated me to invest in and work with a new company called Flexplay Technologies, Inc.

Flexplay developed a truly wonderful idea. They invented a technology that, in essence, makes a DVD self-destruct forty-eight hours (or however many hours it is designed for) after you first play it. (No, it's not like *Mission Impossible*, when the tape burns up. Here a chemical process turns the disk blue at a predetermined point after it is exposed to air, rendering it unreadable by a DVD player.) The technology makes the rental market a one-way street. You go to the store, "rent" a DVD, watch it, and never have to return it. You recycle it with your other plastic garbage. I think it's going to be big.

Now, let's stay on this for a minute. Remember how I said it's dangerous to assume that you're the market? Later on in the chapter, I'm going to warn you to think long and hard before jumping on new technologies, because most of them never catch on. (When was the last time you watched a video on Beta?)

It is fair to ask whether my decision to invest in a DVD technology that self-destructs is an example of the two things I just warned you about: jumping on a technology early and assuming that you are the market. How do I know I'm not dealing with milking machines in Manhattan?

Does everybody have a DVD player?

Well, no.

But you have to look at the technological trends and where those trends are pointing. While I bought my DVD player fairly early, DVD is unquestionably on its way to becoming the standard in the movie-rental industry.

You know intuitively that a better milking machine is probably not a huge market, but a better system for handling video rentals? That's another matter. Obviously, I was going to research the idea to see if it was commercially viable. (Something we will talk about in the last third of the chapter, where we discuss how you can validate the ideas you have come up with by using BPT.) And when I did, the research convinced me that this idea is going to work. It meets a basic need. Returning movies and paying late fees is a pain, and there is no competing technology that eliminates the problem.

Let me make one more point before we move on. A lot of people think the most important part of the innovation process is coming up with the idea. In fact, they talk about it in hushed tones as *the idea*, as if you need to come up with only one and all your problems are solved.

This is completely the wrong way to look at the innovation process.

Ideas are cheap. You can come up with dozens of them in a matter of minutes. For fun, I practice coming up with them in specific categories all the time. I'll try to invent a new sport or a new toy. It's a form of exercise. It helps keep the idea muscle in the brain strong.

So, you can come up with ideas easily. In fact, you can come up with good ideas fairly easily. Just don't focus in on your first one when you've identified a customer need. It's like buying a new house or looking for a new job. The first house you look at may be perfect, or the first job offer might turn out to be ideal, but how will you ever truly know unless you compare it to what else is out there? If you consider four or five, you will probably come up with a better choice. It's exactly the same with ideas.

Always, always have multiple options from which to choose. Your odds of success go through the roof when you have more options. That's why I am such a big believer in BPT. It gives you lots of options.

Does the potential size of the market matter? No, not really, as long as you know its size and accept it. We started DoubleClick in large part because we wanted to go after what we knew was going to be a multibillion-dollar market. Our thinking went like this: We have only so much time during our working lives, and we have the ability to grapple with only one market, one idea, at a time. Given that, we figured it was better to go after a really big need if we were going to start a company from scratch.

But that was our approach. It might not be yours. You might want to go after something smaller, either because that's the natural size of the best idea you come up with, or because it feels right to you. There is no right answer. You have to decide what size need you are going to fill.

Separating Needs from Wants

But how do you know what is something a customer needs and what is something a customer wants—i.e., something the customer thinks would be nice to have but wouldn't go out of his way to buy? How can you tell the difference? The short answer: You'll never know any of this with 100 percent certainty, and that includes distinguishing between a need and a want.

There are a lot of gray areas, especially when it comes to consumers. Is having both a buzzer and an alarm on a clock-radio a need or a want? Seems like an option at first glance. But for people who are heavy sleepers and don't wake up easily, it's a need. The difference between wants and needs is not always clear.

But in many cases, you can identify a business's basic need. They want nicer lighting and more comfortable chairs for their employees. Both things would be nice, but they are wants, not needs.

Sometimes wants transform into needs. Ergonomic keyboards are an example. These used to be wants; now they are needs, to prevent carpal tunnel syndrome and other repetitive stress injuries.

But you don't want to bet on this sort of thing happening. You want to focus on the need, especially in the early stages, when you're introducing something.

To find out whether what you have is a need or a want, ask yourself this:

- Will the idea make the consumer or business money?
- Will it save them money?
- Will it make them more efficient?
- Will it make them more competitive?

If the answer to all those questions is no, then what you are dealing with is likely a want.

But if your idea meets a basic need, and there is an existing technology already in place, then you're on to something big. Where this gets tricky is when customers—people or businesses—don't know they have a need. Did we know we *needed* to boil water in a minute, or to have popcorn two minutes after we took a bag out of the pantry? No, not until the microwave was introduced. In business, did anyone think there was a need to connect PCs to mainframes?

Well, MIS directors certainly didn't. So IBM had just launched its personal computer the summer before, when we started ICC in 1983. Bill Miller, Mike Schier, and I were completely convinced that the PC would revolutionize the way businesses operated. We developed products that allowed businesses to replace their Burroughs terminals with a PC, through terminal emulation software and hardware that we called Intercom. In essence, our product allowed PCs to be tied directly to the corporate mainframe. This concept seems so basic today, but at the time it was viewed as witchcraft.

When we launched the product, nobody called, so we started to call businesses. We must have called a couple hundred companies and received the same answer each time: "PCs will never be allowed into our business, and don't *ever* call me again."

The beauty of trends is they are always obvious in hindsight.

Here's another example. Back in 1994, when I was at DCA, my group was researching another potentially huge trend called groupware, a software product that allowed multiple users, located anywhere, to have group discussions and work on the same document at the same time, essentially capturing organizational knowledge in real time. Pretty cool, huh?

Lotus Notes, an example of what we are talking about, was having great success, and every major company was trying to cash in on the groupware trend. If every major company was pursuing it, the idea had to be huge—or so I thought. We launched our groupware product, called OpenMind (which I humbly contend was the best version out there). Unfortunately, groupware turned out to be more of a buzzword than a trend, and we lost millions of dollars and years of effort.

I actually believe OpenMind could have worked. There's always a need to organize knowledge, but the problem is very difficult to solve, since it's so broad. (What, for example, is "knowledge"?) We created a great product, but our delivery to the market was poor, since it didn't fit well with the company's direction (DCA and Attachmate merged shortly after the release, and the product was essentially abandoned). So the money and people components of what it takes to make a new idea succeed were missing. In addition, Microsoft was about to introduce Exchange, which was then a very nebulous product that reportedly did everything Lotus Notes and OpenMind did plus more.

To this day, I think OpenMind was one of the most interesting and revolutionary products I helped to create. But in business, good art is art that sells, and OpenMind was a black-velvet Elvis painting.

When we launched OpenMind, I received a beautifully framed picture of the product logo as a gift. I keep this picture in my office as a reminder of the thin line between success and failure, and the difference between needs and wants.

Two Other Ways to Discover Needs

There are two other things you can do to improve your ability to determine the difference between a need and want. Both require you to talk in depth with your customers and people you would like to be your customers. During these conversations with these (potential) customers:

1. Spend a lot of time carefully phrasing the way you ask about their needs. Be sure to put your idea in the broadest context possible.
2. Listen for the "of course" answer.

Let me give you a couple of examples.

Let's pretend it's the early 1960s. You're at your neighbor's, watching *The Red Skelton Show* on his black-and-white television. "Color TV is just a fad!" your neighbor insists. What do you think the response would be if you asked, "Would you be willing to pay for television programs?"

The answer would be "No!" Everybody knows that "television" means "free."

But suppose you asked the question this way: "Would you be willing to pay for entertainment?" That answer would be "Of course. We all do that. We all pay money to see movies, sporting events, concerts, and plays."

Your next question, if you were thinking about creating a subscription-based television service, would be: "Would you pay for exclusive forms of entertainment delivered through your television set, if the cost wasn't excessive?"

If you posed the questions that way, you could have predicted the success of HBO, Showtime, subscriptions to the NFL and Major League Baseball seasons, and the like. The initial question you wanted to ask was "Would you pay for entertainment?" not "Would you be willing to pay for television?"

Let me give you two other examples of how important asking the question is when you're trying to figure out potential business or consumer needs.

Prior to the invention of FedEx, if you had asked people whether they needed to get a package someplace overnight, they probably would have said that option would be nice to have. Given such a tepid response, you would have put the idea in the "want" category; and you would have, of course, missed an enormous opportunity.

But if you had asked: "Is there a huge benefit in moving information quickly?" just about everyone would have said, "Of course."

And that "Of course" is the answer you're looking for in confirming that at least one of the ideas you developed during BPT has the potential of turning into a business. It doesn't mean you have a winner. But it is a good indication that you may be on the right path.

One last story to hammer home the point. In early 1995, while we were researching Internet ideas, we came up with the concept of posting and searching résumés online. We went to a number of corporate human-resources vice presidents and told them about our idea. To a person, they said, "Why would I want something like that? Nobody I know uses the Internet." (Remember, this was 1995.) We didn't pursue the thought.

The real question we should have asked was "Would you like easy worldwide access to the best possible candidates?"

I eventually figured that out. Later, when I was offered a chance to invest in the then-fledgling HotJobs, which supports job recruiting on the Internet, I jumped at it. The company and I did extremely well and was acquired by Yahoo! for $466 million during the summer of 2001.

TIME TO MOVE ON

Let's assume you've gone through this process and identified a handful of major needs you love. Great. But you're just a fourth of the way done. You still need to:

- Understand the technology (if you're going to have a big technology component) you'll use to fill the needs you've found;
- Produce a large number of solutions that fill the needs;
- Evaluate your solutions to see if they are the best ones available, given all your other choices; and
- Determine whether people will be willing to pay for it.

Let's look at FedEx again to show what can go horribly wrong if you don't take those two additional steps.

About fifteen years ago, building off the remarkable success of its overnight delivery business, FedEx, in essence, asked businesses and consumers the following question: "If you think getting overnight documents is important, wouldn't it be even better if you could get your important documents there even faster, say within a couple of hours, instead of having to wait overnight?"

That question also got an "of course" answer. So FedEx introduced Zap Mail, a service that typically required you to go down to your local FedEx office with your document. There, an employee would fax it to the FedEx office nearest to the person you wanted to receive it, and another employee would deliver it from there.

The problem was that FedEx didn't pay enough attention to the technology trends at the time. They didn't foresee that fax machines, which existed but were still scarce, or e-mail, which was then virtually unheard of, would make their new service obsolete in a remarkably short time. The changes in technology zapped Zap Mail out of existence.

The point is that when it comes to innovation, you need both sides of the equation: a *need* that fits into where the *technology* is going. Then you must double-check what you have by asking customers if they will pay for your solution, as the final part of this chapter points out.

Must there be a technology component to what you are doing? Almost certainly.

The company that can use technology to its advantage will win.

As we suggested before, needs can be filled without technology. You may decide one day that what you really want to do is open a bookstore in your town that stocks nothing but business titles. That might be one basic need the people in your community have. You could keep the technology component to a minimum, but your ability to grow would be curtailed. The same thing would hold true for a pure service business. The only technology you would need in either case would be basic office equipment—personal computer, printer, fax, phone, etc.—but again, your ability to grow would be limited if that's the only investment in technology that you make.

With many of the products you can think of creating, you'll need a substantial technology component in order to make them work as well as possible.

Technology will be the catalyst for most of the innovative breakthroughs in the future, just as it has been in the past. Not everything is going to be technology-based, but almost everything will have a strong technology component.

The advantages of technology are clear. It will never organize a union; it won't get tired; it can't file frivolous lawsuits (but give the trial lawyers a few more years to crack that one); it doesn't ask for a raise; it won't go on vacation; and it doesn't call in sick. More important, technology has the ability to do things that humans can't or won't, and it does those things well.

Here's another way to think about the importance of technology. Your customers always want things faster, better, cheaper. That requires technology. You know we broke the four-minute mile almost fifty years ago—Roger Bannister did it in 1954—and the times haven't fallen much since then. Human beings aren't getting much faster or much smarter. But technology is.

What if you don't have a technology background? Should you throw this book out? No. But you'll have to team up with someone who does have the necessary expertise. This doesn't mean you can't get started until you do. You can start to identify needs today. You can probably identify many of the technology trends with a minimal amount of research, if you don't have a technological bent. But you absolutely have to partner with someone who knows technology. You must know technology. If you don't know technology, you're in trouble; unless, as I said, all you want to do is start a small service or retail firm. Large ones, like Wal-Mart, have a tremendous technology component, in everything from their point-of-sale terminals to the software and hardware they use to handle inventory and distribution.

Technology is important. That's why we are devoting the second part of the chapter to it.

PART II: THE SIREN CALL OF TECHNOLOGY

The problem with making sure technology is a key part of what you do is clear: You or the people you partner with can get seduced by the technology that's available or just around the corner, and you'll end up heading down a dead-end path.

I am sometimes accused of being cynical about technology. I'm not. But I am skeptical. Sometimes I think technologists are the last people who ought to try to build companies. They are their own worst enemy. They invariably want to use the coolest technology and do things the "right" way, which means they want to do them in a way that is theoretically the most efficient.

But the "right" way frequently doesn't take into account either the way human beings behave or how markets work.

Here's an example. I don't know any technologist who likes America Online (AOL). More than twenty million people in the U.S.

use AOL, making it far and away the most popular Internet service, yet technologists scoff at it, calling AOL "the Internet with training wheels." But ask the technologist which service she would recommend for her own mother, and the answer will be AOL. Technologists don't want to handle the tech-support calls from Mom that will invariably follow if she signs up with someone else. (My mom uses AOL.)

I think the greatest technologists are often the worst ones. They fall in love with the "right" technology more than anyone else, and they do so without regard to whether it will be widely accepted.

We had a guy in our research group at DCA, one of the smartest people I know, and he fell in love with the NeXT computer (which was eventually bought by Apple) and its operating system. His reasons were extremely sound. It's a powerful box. It had the best user interface and operating system. And he hated Microsoft, and he hated Windows. He thought NeXT was the perfect alternative. He wanted us to go in that direction and design products for it.

I told him, "Look, it's not about having the best technology. It's about market share. We want to be offering products in the space where there are the most users. Five years from now, who's going to have the greatest market share? It's not going to be NeXT or even Apple. That's a dead end. We need to be designing products for Windows."

He disagreed and decided to go off on his own and build products for NeXT. It was a mistake. NeXT no longer exists. The market wasn't there.

How do you guard against being seduced by what looks like an extremely appealing technology, especially if you don't have a technology background? It's hard. People, especially technologists, come up with products like Iridium, which would allow you to make phone calls from every point on the globe, and these products sound better than anything out there. In the case of Iridium, when you tell the proponents nobody is going to throw away their old cell phones, they respond by saying, "You junked your phonograph for a CD player, so why wouldn't you trade up to better phone technology?" Of course, the "better" phone technology was a bigger and far more expensive phone. But hey, you could make calls from any jungle in the world.

What do you do in the face of that kind of argument?

You have to remain focused on what is happening in the market.

The whole Wintel phenomenon—the Windows operating system from Microsoft, combined with personal computers containing Intel processors from Intel Corporation—is a great example. For the past twenty years, technologists, like the guy who used to work for us before deciding to devote his career to NeXT, have hated it, but consumers love it. Consumers love Wintel. Now, when consumers stop loving Microsoft or Intel, it will probably be a huge opportunity for a different kind of computer operating system. But until that happens, who cares what's better? It's irrelevant.

Given what we have talked about, it is clear that you want whatever innovation you come up with to take advantage of either an established technology or one you are certain will become an established technology.

But the question is, how long do you wait before embracing one particular technology over another?

If you wait until a technology is truly entrenched, you could be coming late to the party. If you jump too early, you could be betting on a fad, not a trend. Even if you're right, you may use up all your capital before the technology is established. There are a ton of wireless Internet companies and firms based around interactive TV that are going to be out of money long before their markets are firmly in place.

Knowing when to act is probably your toughest call, because some of the greatest opportunities are created early in the trend. How do you get in on the early part? You may not be able to. It all goes back to increasing your probabilities. You have to make sure that the technological trend is actually a trend before you act.

It seems that major shifts in technology—things that throw everything into flux, such as the personal computer or biotech—occur every five to ten years, but certainly no more often than that. The disruptions are so huge that large companies fail to respond quickly. That is understandable. The disruptions, by definition, are going to threaten the way companies are already doing business, and no entrenched organization wants to change the way it does things unless absolutely necessary. That reluctance creates a huge opportunity for you.

What is a good example of a trend you could have jumped on early? The Internet. The Internet always looked to me like it was going to be big; my only question was how big? Why was I so certain? Because the concept of being able to access all information from anywhere at any time was just brilliant. It was revolutionary. The irony today is that the Internet is far bigger than anybody forecasted, yet investors have fallen out of love with it. Sometimes too much attention isn't always a good thing. My mom is so ashamed that I'm an Internet executive that she tells people I'm with the LAPD.

I'll give you a technology trend that I don't think you have to worry about missing: handwriting recognition, in which you can operate your computer by writing things down. They have been working on this forever. It's the same thing with voice recognition. People are convinced that voice will be the primary input device of computers, just like on *Star Trek*. ("Computer, shields up and take us to Rigel Seven, warp three.") But like handwriting, it is terribly inefficient.

IT TAKES TIME

Here is something that might be reassuring if you are worried about missing out on a major technology trend. There has never been a technical breakthrough that changed everything overnight. Things don't change that quickly, which is probably a good thing, simply because people and corporations cannot absorb a lot of change quickly. I think it takes seven to ten years for companies to come to grips with something truly new; I call it the "technology absorption curve." The fastest large-scale integration has probably been the Internet, but the concept was around for decades before it truly caught on in the mid-1990s with the advent of the World Wide Web (which actually began in the early 1990s).

This kind of long lead time turns out to be a good thing, because infrastructure invariably takes a long time to catch up and truly support any new technology. And there is a message in that: Don't bet on infrastructure. In 1995 I was asked to invest in a PDA software company. PDAs (personal digital assistants) are handheld devices that help organize your life and allow you to communicate wirelessly. The success of the company was dependent on two forms of infrastructure: PDAs and wireless. If you don't want to invest in a business that is contingent on one infrastructure developing, you certainly don't want to invest in a business dependent on two. I passed. I thought the chances of success were too small.

People make a classic mistake when they try to determine the probability of success for a company as it relates to technology. Let's stay with the PDA/wireless industry as an example. Back in 1995, there were probably ten major PDAs being developed. Nobody knew who would win, so the probability of picking the right one was, say, 10 percent.

The company I was asked to invest in was also dependent on having a national network of high-speed data. Let's say the probability of that happening was 20 percent (though, in hindsight, it was 0 percent).

At first glance, you might say the company I was asked to help fund had a 10 percent chance of making it (not very good odds). However, the probability was really 2 percent, since the variables were independent. (Here's why. You have a one-in-ten chance of picking the right PDA. And even if you select the right one, there is only a one-in-five chance of the infrastructure being created. The math looks like this: 10 percent × 20 percent = 2 percent chance of success. When the odds are fifty to one against you, you don't want to bet.)

When I tell people to be wary of betting on infrastructure, I get a pretty predictable response: "Isn't that a chicken-and-egg problem?" they ask. "You're telling me that if I want to invest in a new technology—either with my money or by trying to innovate within that space—I shouldn't because it's going to take the infrastructure a long time to support it, twenty years in the case of cell phones. What am I supposed to do in the interim?"

Great question. Here is the blunt answer: If your business is based on high-speed wireless access being available to everyone, you're out of business. But if your business is to be a provider of the service, you've got a shot, since infrastructure always has to come before applications. For example, the big knock against Flexplay is that video on demand will displace the need to get the physical media—you'll simply play it on your TV through high-speed cable access. Of course, cable companies have been promising high-speed access for fifteen years. Wireless companies have been promising national high-speed wireless access for ten years. Just because a company promises something doesn't make it so. I think Flexplay has a real shot, since it solves a need, one that existing companies have only talked about filling. You'll never have to pay an outrageous late fee, and you'll never have to return a DVD again.

There are different stages in the development of a technology, and you can be successful at each. To me, whoever the leader is in each of the segments as the technology is evolving will be a winner.

Here's another way to think about all this. At any given moment, there are a number of concurrent trends that will end up defining our world. These trends hopefully represent the best of what is happening with technology and business practices. The older the trend, the easier it is to recognize. For example, nobody would argue that the PC, globalization, networking, and the Internet don't represent huge trends that have transformed every corner of our world.

Still, I would suggest caution when it comes to putting all your resources against the latest technology early on. The early stages of a technological trend are extremely difficult to recognize and equally hard to distinguish from fads or hype (the first time I saw the Web in the early 1990s, I thought it was slow and worthless). True, huge trends create huge opportunities, and the earlier you recognize a trend, the better your chances are of creating a huge company. But the earlier you move, the higher the risk that you're hopping not on a trend but on a fad. When I look back at why we failed with a venture—and as I mentioned in the last chapter, I have failed at a few—it usually involved an incorrect reading of the tea leaves. I moved too early, not too late. The Open-Mind groupware is a prime example. If we had started our first company, the one that connected PCs to mainframes, just one week earlier, we would have run out of money. That's how close we cut it.

But don't you have to be the first to market? A lot of people think so. It's even called First Mover Advantage. Are they right? Well, if you are first, and if you have the best product, best management, and lots of money, you definitely will win if you are first to market. It's just that moving first doesn't guarantee success, especially if you're taking the wrong approach with the wrong team.

THE MORAL: DON'T JUMP TOO SOON

As I said, I wouldn't call myself a cynic, but I am highly skeptical of new technologies and the business concepts associated with them. People are often surprised by my skepticism and my suggestion that they should be extremely skeptical as well. They want to know how companies become market leaders if they don't jump on the next hot technology that comes along.

This gets back to my whole notion of focus. You can focus on only one opportunity at a time. Out of a hundred hot technologies that come along, probably two or three will establish themselves as industry-changing. The tough job is trying to figure out what those two or three winners will be.

If you pursue anything that moves, you'll never have the time or resources to find and focus on your idea.

A HUNDRED THOUSAND LEMMINGS
CAN'T BE WRONG

Ignoring what appears to be the *next big thing* is difficult, because we want to believe that technology can solve all of our problems. That's the great allure. Any new technology that promises to deliver on this belief will find a lot of suckers.

Sometimes I think there's an inverse correlation between the early embrace of a technology by major companies and its ultimate success. And always beware of excessive buzzwords! I tried to prove that point one day with a prank, although I'll admit it didn't have the kind of results I thought it would.

When DCA bought ICC back in 1992, I became responsible for the creation of new products at DCA. I love April Fool's Day and decided to play a joke on my new employer—always a good way to start a job. I sent out an e-mail to all employees, inviting them to see a product prototype we had created. (The product was mythical. I made it up. But I was the only one who knew that.) I basically took every buzzword in the industry and put them together in the description of my revolutionary product. I told them I had created a palm-held mobile video-conferencing system (which is still impossible a decade later).

To my surprise, there was a roomful of people waiting to see this "radically new breakthrough" device. Before I began, I had a person stand on a chair and hold the device in an awkward position (I told everyone who had gathered that the satellite signal was not particularly strong in the building).

I was convinced that I had a terrific way to show people why they shouldn't be seduced by things that sounded too good to be true. I proceeded with my presentation, which ended with a slide that asked, "What do you get when you combine all the industry buzzwords into a single device?"

All the next slide said was "A roomful of suckers."

By the time I was done, I was laughing so hard that I nearly wet my pants, but nobody else got the joke—and these were all smart people. I had to tell them explicitly that I made everything up as an April Fool's joke to underscore the idea that we all get suckered by cool technology. Even then some didn't believe that the idea for a palm-held mobile video-conferencing system wasn't true.

The point I was trying to make then is the same one I'm trying to make now: Don't smash your ship on the rocks as a result of being lured by the sirens of technology.

If you've decided to downplay technology, and to emphasize applying trends to needs, make sure a trend is a trend and not a fad or a mistaken idea. In other words, don't be lured by the sirens of trends.

IT'S NOT THAT HARD

I don't believe in conspiracies, but I believe that research and consulting companies, as well as most business school professors, have a running contest to see who can create the most new words.

Back in 1995, there was a view that the Internet was all about "disintermediation." (I knew this was a new word, since my spell checker was confused by it. If anybody knows who created the word, as well as the theory that we are all going to be disintermediated out of existence, please e-mail me at koconnor@kojjee.com.)

When we were out looking for money for DoubleClick, I was asked repeatedly if we were worried about being disintermediated into bankruptcy. After all, these people wondered, "the Internet is about disintermediation, won't you be disintermediated?"

"Of course not," I said, although I had no clue what I was being asked. I thought they were referring to a disease. I discovered that "disintermediation" means that on the Internet, everyone will cut out the intermediaries—or the middleman—and sell directly to the ultimate consumer or business. Rather than go to a grocery store, you would buy products directly from the manufacturer. I know it sounds silly, but this was a big belief back then.

Companies that were historically dependent on retailers jumped on this idea hard. Finally, they figured, they would have the chance to put the screws to the companies selling their products.

While I understood why this idea would make some companies happy, I thought then—and I know now—that the people who endorsed the concept got it completely backward. I always viewed the Internet as being about "reintermediation," which is another made-up word, one that I might be responsible for. (Sorry.)

Reintermediation is the word I would use for replacing an inefficient distribution system with a more efficient one, one built around the Internet. Many of the largest Internet companies (Amazon, Yahoo!, eBay, DoubleClick) are all reintermediators. They are all (efficient) middlemen.

Many companies that pursued the disintermediation theory ended up with a great disaster on their hands.

Every airline thought they could get rid of the intermediaries. Their model of the future was selling directly to the customer. You would call them up, or go to their website, and buy the tickets directly. No more travel agents, and no more commissions paid by the airlines to those travel agents.

Travelocity and Expedia are two of the most successful new companies, and they act as reintermediaries. Why? That's easy to answer. Are you going to trust United or American to give you the best airfare?

Hell, no! You'll go to to someone who can search out the lowest possible price for you.

Procter & Gamble and Unilever both experimented with selling products directly. Can you imagine shopping at fifty different stores (or websites) just to buy your groceries? Of course not. You'd go to an intermediary, be it a supermarket, drugstore, or online grocer.

We'll never get to the mythical "frictionless economy" that Bill Gates envisioned, but we will get rid of most of the friction through highly efficient, technology-rich reintermediaries.

And that is the point. People used to talk a lot about the difference between the old economy and the new economy, maintaining that the new economy would be substantially better because it would be based on new technologies. But framing the argument in terms of new economy versus old economy misses the point. The improvements will come from companies that can figure out how to use new technologies to innovate efficiency. New (-economy) companies can do that. But so-called old-economy companies can do that, as well.

Disintermediation was a fad. It is not a trend.

NOW THAT YOU KNOW WHAT TO LOOK FOR

Okay, all the warnings and background are out of the way. I feel like I just explained that you're in a minefield and you want to know where the mines are. Unfortunately, that's impossible to tell you. But hey, at least you know it's a minefield and you need to be careful. It is now time to use BPT to identify all the technologies out there that could help you satisfy your target market needs.

Once you have come with a list—which could be fifty or seventy-five technologies long—use the process we talked about in the last chapter to winnow that list down to a handful, say six, that look the most promising.

Then take the most promising technologies and plot them against the most promising needs you came up with earlier.

Your table should look like this:

	1 **Tech 1**	**2** **Tech 2**	**3** **Tech 3**	**4** **Tech 4**	**5** **Tech 5**	**6** **Tech 6**
A Need 1						
B Need 2		B2				
C Need 3						
D Need 4						
E Need 5						
F Need 6					F5	

Then go through the exercise that we talked about at the beginning of the chapter. Apply each of the technologies to each of the needs and attempt to brainstorm solutions (not every technology can be applied to every need). In the box labeled B2, you would apply technology 2 to need 2, and in the box labeled F5, you would apply technology 5 to need 6.

Obviously, you could end up with hundreds of potential products or services. (If you came up with only eight in each box, you'd end up with a total of 288.) How do you reduce that list to a manageable number? By using the same winnowing-down process we talked about in the last chapter: You number each idea, divide by three to arrive at the number of votes each person gets, vote, and take the top three to six solutions. At the end of the chapter, I will show you the example of this that led to the creation of DoubleClick.

You want to end up with the best ideas once you have applied technology to needs.

When you have narrowed down the list to that point, it is time to find out if there is truly a market for your idea.

DETERMINING THE VIABILITY OF WHAT YOU HAVE

Let's stop for a minute and make sure we know where we are.

After applying technology to needs, and winnowing down the result, you have come up with what looks like three to six very promising ideas—efficient solutions to real problems.

The next step is to determine if any of those ideas are commercially viable. This validation step will take some time and effort. You need to figure out a number of different things:

- Does your idea solve a real need?
- Are there competing products? If so, what makes yours overwhelmingly superior?
- What do your prospects or customers think about what you have? You already know you've identified a need, but will they pay for a solution? What exactly do they want your product or service to do? What features do they need? What features don't they need?
- Who is your likely competition? Can you stave them off?
- Is there a reason the market isn't being served?
- Is the market big enough?
- What do the "experts" think? (Hint: Their opinion may not matter.)

These are tough questions, but you have to answer every one, because your goal at this point is to narrow your focus to the *one* idea you'll focus on to build your company.

> **Ultimately, you can pursue only one idea. The rest you need to throw away and forget. Don't worry, ideas are cheap! After all, you came up with dozens of them during BPT.**

Because those questions are so important, let's deal with them one at a time.

1. **Does your idea solve a real need?** There are way too many start-ups—and that includes the ones that begin life inside an established company—that have a cool technology but don't actually fix a serious problem. The idea of creating a cellular communication system that would let you talk to anyone—whether you were on top of Mount Everest or in the middle of the Gobi Desert—was incredibly cool. The problem was, you could probably count the number of people who needed it and were willing to pay for it on the fingers of one hand. That's why Iridium, backed by many world-class companies (including, most notably, Motorola), went bankrupt. Obviously, you don't want to go down that path. You want to provide an efficient solution for a real need, something like laser printers, which not only produced cleaner printed copies than the old dot-matrix printers, but produced them faster. Cool technology, and/or stringing together multiple buzzwords, doesn't cut it; you must solve a need. I'm repeating myself, I know, but I'm doing it for a reason. The point needs to register.

2. **Are any other products addressing the customer problem?** Often engineers, and others, come up with the proverbial better mousetrap. People say, "We can do a better version of the product (or service) currently being provided by market leader, company X, so we'll win." Think of the dozens of companies who have tried to take on Microsoft's suite of office products, such as Microsoft Word. Be very, very, very careful if you are tempted to go down that road. First, "better" is a pretty nebulous term, and any good marketer worth his salt can obfus-

cate what is truly best for the customer. A well-entrenched competitor has the advantage of reputation and trust, something a start-up, or a new product in a new market from an established firm, is seriously lacking. You can't be incrementally different and expect the customer to throw away what she has in order to go with you.

Second, don't underestimate the intelligence of your competitor. You don't have the monopoly on IQ. If your idea is great, the established competition will simply "borrow" it. As Mark Twain supposedly said, "I know a good idea when I steal it." Simply improving an existing product will not work. Do you know anyone who does not use Microsoft Word?

3. **What do prospects or customers think?** Go out and ask real live prospects for reactions to your ideas. Verify that you are solving a problem that they perceive to be a problem. Let me add a word of caution: It may not always be possible to ask them. If you are in the early part of a trend, talking to customers will not do you much good, since they probably haven't even recognized they have a need. When we started ICC in 1983, no manager of information systems believed that he would ever have PCs in his organization. Our leap of faith was betting that MIS people wouldn't have the final say over whether PCs would creep into the organization. So, we truly didn't take what they told us seriously. For us, the question was: If PCs were in the organization, would the MIS manager want to connect all these new personal computers to the corporate mainframe? The answer? Of course they would. They wouldn't have a choice. What employee would want two computers on her desk?

We encountered the same sort of problem when we were researching what would ultimately become DoubleClick. Back when we started talking to advertisers in 1995, none of them had any interest in advertising on the Web. Why would they? Nobody was using the Web. Yet. I spent a lot of time with advertisers and ad agencies to better understand their fundamental problems, which are fairly simple: Advertisers want to target their message and see how their ads influence consumer behavior. We knew we could solve this problem on the Web; our only issue was, would the Internet become a large medium? In this, we had no doubt. The point? If you're early in the game, prospects might not be able to give you valid feedback. They might not truly understand what you have.

4. **Who is your most likely competition, and is the market defensible?** If you don't have a competitor today, who is most likely to enter your market tomorrow? Both Dwight Merriman and I had spent many years in the software industry, where Microsoft was slowly taking over each interesting segment. As he and I set off to start a technology company, our biggest fear was—not surprisingly—Microsoft. Even though one of our original ideas was good—a software tool that would help design websites—we didn't pursue it. We knew that Microsoft would need to own the market. (Surprisingly, it ignored this area for a long time and ended up buying a start-up, Vermeer, which became the basis of their FrontPage product. But we didn't know that would happen. We thought they would continue expanding into horizontal markets, such as Web design.)

5. **Is there a reason the market isn't being served?** Although your idea may seem obvious, don't assume that anybody has figured it out. Around 1986 or so, while I was at ICC, a customer told me he wanted his company PCs to dial in to their local area network. I told him that didn't sound like too hard a problem and I would find him a solution. After looking everywhere, and talking to all the logical companies, I couldn't find anyone who offered a product that would let you do it. Of course, we all dial in to LANs today, but back then it would have been considered a miracle. We spent months agonizing over whether we should pursue the product, since it was too obvious. Eventually, we ended up moving ahead, and I developed the remote LAN node (RLN). RLN was a reasonably successful product, though it could have been far more successful if we had started earlier and attacked the market more

aggressively. We didn't because we were convinced that everyone would soon see what we did, then come and take the market away from us. The experience convinced me the old adage is right: The best ideas are the obvious ones.

6. **Is the market big enough?** With ICC, we executed very well and ended up with 95 percent of the market. Unfortunately, the market was around $50 million a year and shrinking. Only so many people needed to connect PCs to Burroughs and Sperry mainframes. Ironically, this was great for us, since we were the only company offering solutions to companies that had Burroughs and Sperry mainframes. But as companies migrated away from mainframes, there was less and less need for our product. We kept that thought in mind when we were searching for the company that would become DoubleClick. We wanted to pursue only massive markets that wouldn't shrink over time.

7. **Be wary of the experts.** Okay, I admit that I will quote the expert whenever her opinion agrees with mine. But to be serious, I try to use analyst reports as simply another data input or opinion. The real point about experts is that you need to become one. If you are innovating within an existing company, you better be more expert than the expert. You need to be the expert not just in your company but also in your industry. Remember, you'll be betting your life and money on your company; the experts aren't. If this doesn't work out, they can always become an expert at something else. You may not have that luxury.

You Can't Prove the Unprovable

Sizing your market is important, however. I think market forecasting is where most people fall down. They break out the Excel spreadsheets and create these complex models that show *exactly* how the market will unfold, based on expert predictions.

Remember that forecasts are always wrong. You're going to be either too high or too low.

To me, markets are small, big, or huge. Small markets you ignore if you are a start-up; or hand off to one of your divisions if you are an established firm. Big markets are what you go after if you can't find a huge market.

Huge markets are the grand slams that we all dream about hitting. Using some basic intuition, you can size a market reasonably quickly to find out if you are dealing with a small, big, or huge market. You don't need strategic planning to figure out the size, because no one truly knows how big it is going to be.

I have always been fascinated by the Heisenberg Uncertainty Principle in physics. According to HUP, no matter how hard you try, you can't measure all the quantities of a system with complete certainty. The uncertainty comes from the measuring instruments you use. No matter how good they are, they are always a little bit off—and it can be the smallest little bit imaginable. With forecasting, the uncertainty comes from your inability to know what is going to happen in the future.

No matter how hard you try, no matter how much time you spend, no matter how much money you throw at it, you will never be able to determine the future with certainty. Spending 10 percent of your resources on the problem may get you to 50 percent certainty, but spending ten times more will increase your certainty by only a small amount more. Unfortunately, that will delude you into thinking you have obtained complete certainty, that you know exactly how the market is going to unfold.

Indeed, it was all this studying that frustrated me with traditional strategic planning techniques in the first place and led to what became BPT. It seemed we always got almost all of the great ideas on day one and the rest of the time was spent on validating them, researching, forecasting, and creating complex net-present-value analysis based on the probabilities that certain events would happen. In other words, once we captured all the good ideas, we wasted enormous amounts of effort and time justifying the fact that we had gotten all the good ideas.

I think the biggest mistake companies or individuals make during strategic planning is trying to prove the unprovable. Essentially, you are trying to predict the future. We would spend months looking for "facts" (other predictions) from the "experts" to "prove" that we were right. What a waste of valuable time and money.

> **You will never know the future for certain. Understand that and embrace it. Get into the market early with an imperfect product. Once you're actively in the market, you'll learn plenty about what it will take to be successful, and you'll tweak your product and strategy as a result.**

As General Patton knew, executing a less-than-perfect plan today is far better then the perfect plan never executed.

> **When people spend a great deal of time trying to forecast the future, they fool themselves into thinking that all those forecasts represent a real level of certainty. They no longer see it as a forecast; they see it as fate. That is a prescription for failure.**

All that overthinking reminds me of an old joke that one of my professors told us to underscore the difference between engineers and mathematicians. You can tell it from either a man's or a woman's point of view. Since I am a guy, you'll hear it from the male perspective. Here's the joke:

An engineer and a mathematician are at a party when a beautiful woman enters the room. They try to figure out the best way to approach her. The mathematician says, "If I go halfway across the room and then halfway again, and again and again, I will never reach her. So I'll stay here." The engineer listens to the mathematician's argument and says, "Hell, I'll get close enough to count."

Be an engineer. You don't have to get it perfect; you just need to be close enough.

YOU STILL MAY NOT HAVE IT

Hopefully, after you have completely researched the top three to six ideas that came out of BPT, you'll find one that you're convinced represents the best opportunity. But as we talked about in the last chapter, you shouldn't feel obligated to pursue any of the ideas if you don't feel they are viable. If you don't have overwhelming confidence in the list, go back to the beginning of this chapter and start over.

Will there be a tip-off that a seemingly terrific idea is not going to work? Sure, some of it may be quantitative: The market is too small; there are too many competitors; nobody wants the product. Sometimes it's qualitative. You end up saying, "I'm not excited about the idea and don't want to waste my life working on it." Whatever the reason, start again.

You'll know when you have the idea. You'll become obsessed. You won't be able to sleep. I felt this way when we came up with Double-Click and the other ventures I've been involved with. You will, too.

A lot of people believe all ideas come out of nowhere, a sort of divine inspiration. I call these folks the fatalists. However, I believe that we make our own luck. If you create a lot of opportunities, you can make an educated choice as to which opportunity is best. I'm a determinist.

PUTTING ALL THIS TO WORK

In the last chapter, we devoted a lot of time to BPT. And there is a reason. It's important. It is the best way I know to force innovation. The best way to, as the subtitle of this book says, create something out of nothing.

Let me give a mini case study of how all these factors can come together successfully. We took everything that we just talked about and applied it when we started DoubleClick. We followed BPT completely. Let me tell you what happened.

In 1995, Dwight Merriman and I set out to create a technology company. That was the only thing we were certain of. That was our one definite goal. We were wide open to any idea. The prospect of starting a company that would take advantage of what was happening out in the marketplace was very exciting, and though we didn't have a clue about what kind of company we wanted to create, we knew we needed to focus quickly. There were thousands of people like us, going off on their own to create businesses that could take advantage of all the technology advances that seemed to be occurring daily. To help figure out what we should do, we used BPT and started at the beginning.

As we have discussed in detail, when it comes to innovation, you need to find a customer need and then, in the best of all possible worlds, figure out how to apply technology to it to make your solution more efficient. You can start from either side: with the need or with the technology. While starting with the need will usually yield more options, Dwight and I began where we were most comfortable—the technology.

It appeared to us that there were going to be four technologies with a chance to be huge in the years ahead:

• CD-ROM/multimedia
• Internet
• Wireless, remote and mobile
• Distributed systems, or computing power that eliminates the need for mainframes. The power of spreading complex applications across many computers vastly exceeds the power of any single computer, including mainframes.

We then used the same kind of grid I've talked about and plotted those four technologies against the seven needs that we thought showed the most promise. The needs revolved around:

• Security
• Entertainment

- Education
- Telecom
- Information access
- Electronic commerce
- E-mail

Here is a partial list of the actual results from our work. The thing to remember when you examine this grid is that many of the ideas—like "Job search/résumés"—were repeated across all four of the technologies.

In the end, we came up with more than eighty possible product ideas.

As I look back on this list, a few thoughts strike me. First, we were able to identify very early on (remember, we went through this exercise back in the early part of 1995, when the Web essentially didn't exist) many of the major trends that would come to dominate the Internet.

Second, we were completely wrong about the CD-ROM industry's development. At the time, dial-up access to the Internet was still incredibly sluggish (back then, 9,600 baud, a hundred times slower than today's standard, was a luxury, and the vast majority of schools and businesses had no Internet connection at all), and we didn't believe that it could quickly overcome the bandwidth constraints.

We were wrong about that. But fortunately, we were right about the assumptions that led to DoubleClick.

Here, in a nutshell, is how the company came about.

As we narrowed down the eighty ideas to a handful, using the BPT process, one thing became clear. We were going to go into the Internet space. Those ideas kept getting the most votes during the winnowing-down part of BPT. The Internet idea that Dwight and I liked the most was aggregating websites and offering people a subscription that would cover them all.

At the time, AOL dominated the online market. With AOL, you got access and content. Our belief was that access and content would split and fragment into smaller and smaller parts—essentially, Internet

USER'S BUSINESS NEEDS

Technology	Security	Entertainment	Education
CD-ROM *Multimedia*	Criminal case files Software distribution	Best of… Workout bike	Focus on toddlers
Internet	Encryption gateway	Networked cameras CDs Porn Pictures Forums Hobbies Personal Web servers	Classes Testing Encyclopedias Course scheduling Tutors
Wireless, remote and mobile	Disk encryption	Games, crossword puzzles Diet and workout w/pulse and blood-pressure attachments	
Distributed Systems		One-way video for porn	

Simple Telecom	Information Access	Electronic Commerce	E-mail

	Web/Net news
	Government
	  public domain
	Public-domain
	  books
	Home prices
	College
	  applications
	Jobs/résumés
		Software
		  distribution
		Music
			Address book

Wiring Atlanta
Notice of
  incoming
  e-mails
	Movie reviews
	411
	CD reviews
	Web server
	Electronic ad
	  agency
	Family Internet
	  access
	City maps
	Jobs/résumés
	Real estate
	  listings
		Video store w/
		  home delivery
		Travel agency
		Fax service
		Dating/personal
		  ads
		E-mall
		  auction house
		Term papers
		Video cameras	

One in box	Web browsers Internet access	Fax Transcribing voice mail	
	Corporate Web cache	Fax service Archive service Internet bank Mall owner	

service providers (ISPs) and websites. When they did, we believed, there would be thousands of subscription-based websites (boy, were we wrong) and that no one would want to sign up for dozens of subscriptions for multiple sites. We figured they'd want one-stop shopping.

So our initial idea was to act like your local cable company. We would bundle together a number of channels (subscription-based websites) and offer you, the customer, access to all of them for a fee. For one price, you'd get unlimited access to sites X, Y, and Z. For an added premium, you'd get additional access to better sites. (Like a cable-TV subscriber, for a basic monthly charge of $X, you'd get fifty or so basic channels. Pay a premium, and you'd get the basic channels plus a movie channel or two, a sports package, etc.)

While researching our Internet concept, we kept running into a belief that we grew to share: that advertising, rather than subscriptions, would be the main economic driver for publishers on the Web. We became increasingly uncomfortable with the idea of getting people to pay for subscriptions to websites, and we eventually abandoned the concept after expending months of effort.

But in the process, we had discovered an even better idea. On the day we decided to abandon the subscription network, Dwight said, "Why don't we aggregate websites for advertisers rather than subscribers? We could create an advertising network."

Boom!

The proverbial lightbulb went on over our heads, and we knew we had *the idea*. We went upstairs that night (we were working in my basement in Atlanta at the time) and I told Nancy, my wife, that the search was over. I finally had a job again. We never looked back. It turns out that the insight was exactly right. DoubleClick has become *the* global Internet marketing solutions company. We focus on creating solutions that make Internet marketing work for websites that carry ads, and for the Web advertisers who place their messages there. As we had set out to do, we put technology at the heart of the operation.

ONE LAST THOUGHT

You may have noticed that up until now, I haven't mentioned anything about making money as you search for ways to create innovations. That was deliberate. I think profits are a byproduct, not a goal, of innovation. Henry Ford believed that the most important thing a company could do was provide a valuable product for the customer. If it did that, Ford said, profits would follow, and I absolutely agree. For a company to say, "Our goal is to make profits" is meaningless. The point of a business is to solve a problem and do it in the best possible way. If you do that, an overwhelming number of people will buy from you; you'll get a huge market share; and you'll make lots of money. I can't think of a company that has a large market share that isn't insanely profitable.

SUMMARY

We are going to do this chapter summary a bit differently. We'll quickly review the process to make sure you come up with as many solutions to customer needs as possible.

Then, since there are four primary variables you have to be concerned with—needs, technology, solutions, and finding out if you have a viable idea once you apply needs to technology—we are going to divide the summary into four additional parts: needs, technology, solutions, and evaluating the solutions that result when you apply technologies to needs.

First, how you go about it.

The Process

1. **BPT needs.** Using the Brainstorming Prioritization Technique, identify as many commercial needs as possible.

2. **BPT technology.** Do the same thing to come up with technologies that you might want to employ to solve those needs.

3. **BPT solutions.** Apply each of those technologies to every one of the needs.

4. **Research your top three to six solutions.** Come up with the best possible one.

5. **Repeat, if necessary.** If you don't like any of the ideas, go back to step 1.

Now let's take each of the variables one at a time.

Needs

1. **Who is your customer?** (Or your potential customer?) This is absolutely the first thing you have to determine before you even think about what they might need.

2. **Don't limit your search for ideas.** You know more than you think you do. Certainly look for ideas where you work now, but also consider opportunities you encounter when you're a consumer or just relaxing.

3. **Remember, you are not necessarily the market.** Just because you like chocolate-covered lima beans doesn't mean the world does. It is always dangerous to assume you are the market.

Technology

1. **Don't be too early.** Before you commit, make sure a technology trend is indeed a trend, something that will last. You don't have the resources to chase every hot technology.

2. **Don't bet on infrastructure.** It always takes far longer to develop than anyone thinks.

3. **The best technology may not be the best** … from the consumer's point of view. Always go with what the consumers like, not the choice of technologists. The market for what they like may not be big enough.

Solutions: Testing what you have

1. **You may not have the answer.** It is more than possible that you will devote months of your life to what you were sure was *the answer* only to

find out it wasn't. Don't try to make a less-than-perfect solution work. Try again.

2. **Will someone pay for what you have?** That is the ultimate test.

3. **Don't worry about profits.** If you are truly satisfying a need efficiently, profits will come.

CHAPTER

4

DEVELOPING THE STRATEGY

If you come to a fork in the road, take it.
—LAWRENCE PETER (YOGI) BERRA

If I weren't convinced that no one would read it, I would have called this chapter "Writing the Business Plan," because that is really what we're going to talk about here. I understand why people would be inclined to skip over something like "Constructing the Perfect Business Plan for Your Organization," or even "Business Plans for Dummies," because most of the business plans out there are long, deadly dull, and never used.

The problem isn't with the idea of creating a business plan; it is with the people who create them. They fill the document with buzzwords ("We are going to maximize the value of the fully integrated supply chain while disintermediating the traditional distribution channels") when simple English will do ("We are going to sell directly to consumers"). There is more minutiae then you can believe ("We are going to hire a sales manager in the second quarter; have twenty-three salespeople and nine support staff in place by the end of Q3; and have eighteen fully executed marketing relationships under way by the end of our first fiscal year, when people will be making 1,217 phone calls per day"). Invariably, there are sales and earning projections going out ten years, based on assumptions that even my eight-year-old wouldn't take seriously. No wonder no one wants to read business plans.

That's too bad, because when it's done right, a business plan is just that: a plan or strategy that describes clearly and concisely how the important aspects of the business will be run. It doesn't need to go into the detail of how many people will be working in the CFO's office forty-two months from now, but a good plan sets out the corporate line of attack, what the company is and is not going to do in the years ahead.

A solid business plan is a blueprint. It shows everyone—potential investors, senior management, and employees—what the organization will be all about for the foreseeable future. It lays out how you'll turn your idea into a reality: how you'll create it, fund it, sell it, and staff it over the next couple of years. The plan will show everyone that you are going to focus on only the things you need to do to be successful.

You can't do a credible job of predicting the future beyond a couple of years. The farther out you go, the fuzzier the picture gets. But you can map how you'll approach the market over the next twelve to thirty-six months.

Specifically, the business plan is the place where you spell out:

1. What problem you are going to solve
2. How your product or service solves it best
3. How you'll bring your product or service to market

Business plans are the documents that reduce the answers to those three questions into writing. They are the place where you clearly capture the strategy of your business, the direction your organization will be heading in the years ahead.

It's like playing chess. You're considering not only your next move but also what will happen—or could happen—three or four or five moves down the line. Are there obvious things that could destroy you or hurt you? What are the three or four things you have to do that will really separate you from the competition? These are the sorts of issues you need to address. We will go through all this step by step.

People tend to spend either no time or too much time on strategy. Spending no time is just dumb. But spending too much time to make sure you get all your ducks in a row can be worse. You'll never have all the answers. You need to get to market quickly so you can learn. Figure out what is important, then move on it. Just have your ducks facing in the same direction and get in the game.

This is what I find so admirable about Microsoft's "incremental innovation" approach. They create a product and get it out in the marketplace as soon as they can. Think about their first version of Windows or Word or PowerPoint. They were all terrible. And when Explorer came out, it was far inferior to Netscape. They know the product can be improved, and they count on the feedback from the market, from real customers, to help them improve it. They don't wait until the product is perfect to launch. No one can afford to wait that long.

Procter & Gamble has been taking a similar approach for years. They get in the market and learn from the feedback. How many improvements have there been in Crest toothpaste or Tide detergent over the years?

Microsoft and P&G are exceptions, though. Products are always too late for market. The reason is that the engineers who are creating the products see themselves as artists, so they want to create perfection before they enter the market. That is just silly. Get the product out there, and let the market tell you what is perfect and what isn't.

Now, of course, the product can't be a complete piece of garbage. You've worked too hard—quickly but hard—to achieve a product that you think covers most of a customer's needs. Don't waste time trying to get it perfect. Remember General Patton's approach: A good plan now is better than a perfect one later.

PAY ATTENTION TO THE NONBARKING DOG

Strategy is not just determining the 1 percent you will do. It is also figuring the 99 percent you won't.

For example, at DoubleClick, we used to "rep" the advertising for two of the largest websites on the market, Excite and Netscape. That meant our sales guys would go around and try to get ads to run on those sites.

As part of the deal, we insisted that in moving forward, Excite and Netscape had to use our new DART technology (the real basis of our company), which would help them measure the effectiveness of the ads because it was a benefit to advertisers. We figured that would be a big advantage, and everyone would win.

But they refused to use DART, though we were firm that they had to, if they wanted us to keep selling ads for them. The result? We lost the business. But that ultimately turned out to be a good thing, because we killed our repping business to create our own advertising network based on the DART technology.

Another example of our determining what we were not going to do occurred soon after DoubleClick first started, when many people approached us to do joint ventures internationally. We said no. We had to stay focused on the U.S. first. As we told them, only half joking, we wanted to make all of our mistakes domestically at first and not replicate them all over the world.

Not surprisingly, BPT is an excellent tool when you're figuring out what your strategy should (and should not) be. There are a hundred different ways to position your company; a hundred features you can put in your product; a hundred different ways to get your product to market. Use BPT at each step to figure out which approach is best for what you are trying to accomplish. (I'll give you specific examples as we go along.)

Anytime you have to produce lots of options, use BPT.

When you gather people in a room to undertake the BPT process that will lead to your positioning, promotion, pricing, and placement, make sure your senior executives are there, since they'll be responsible for executing whatever strategy you develop. You'd be surprised how many times they are left out of the process once a company or division starts to grow. That's like leaving out the general contractor while planning your new house. It doesn't make sense.

WHAT YOU ARE AIMING FOR

People often treat their strategy document like a list of hot-tub rules. You know those rules. You've seen them posted by the pool at nice hotels. Invariably, there will be a sign that says, "No drinking in the hot tub, no horseplay, and no children under eighteen," and we all drink beer and let our kids play in the hot tub.

Don't treat your strategy document the same way. You don't have to treat it like the Ten Commandments, with no room for interpretation. But you do have to take it seriously, very seriously. The goal of your business plan is to create the definitive strategy that will direct your company in the years ahead.

We used BPT to develop the business plans for both ISS and DoubleClick. Even years after their creation, the business plans of both companies helped keep them focused on where they were going.

In the first year of DoubleClick, we met with Lawrence Calcano, an investment banker from Goldman Sachs. The meeting was completely premature, since we were a long way from going public, but I wanted to make sure we'd be well positioned to do so in the future. A couple of years later, we met with Lawrence again to begin the IPO process. Lawrence pulled out our business plan and was blown away: We had actually done what the business plan said we would do in developing specific products that would help advertisers target their message. We hit product schedules. We identified future products that we ultimately developed. We projected the market amazingly well. We were very close to the financial numbers we forecasted, and the investment bankers were amazed. (Doing what you say you'll do is apparently a rare event.) I believe we were able to accomplish what we set out to do thanks to our obsessive desire to focus on only the things that needed to get done. We didn't allow the company to get distracted. The business plan was key in establishing that primary focus.

This is the kind of result you want. It's why you need to be explicit about what you are setting out to do. As you go along, the strategy may change around the edges. If your strategy was to create the world's largest pizza company, and over time you shift from selling deep-dish pies to thin crusts because the thin-crust market got larger or grew faster than you anticipated, that's fine; it's to be expected. But it's not like you set out to be the world's biggest pizza company and a week from Tuesday, you're selling dog food. That's a big strategy change. If you deviate too far from your initial strategy, something is terribly wrong.

> Your strategy should be a living document, like the U.S. Constitution: all-encompassing, hard to change, but flexible enough to evolve as major opportunities or crises warrant. But remember, the world doesn't change that quickly. Your strategy shouldn't, either.

At the risk of repeating myself, remember the central message of this book: Concentrate on what needs to be done and ignore everything else. Concentrating on strategy is a need. You need to focus in on the right idea from the beginning. In the idea-generation stage—before you've committed any resources in an attempt to turn your idea into a reality—changing direction is like turning around a rowboat. It doesn't take much effort. Changing strategy once you are under way is like turning around the *Queen Mary.* You waste time, money, and resources. Your passengers aren't happy. (Plus, the whole harbor sees your mistake.) That's why you need to be clear on your direction from the beginning. As the adage goes, if you don't know where you're going, any route can take you there. You need to chart your course from the beginning, and that clarity of thinking needs to be reflected in your business plan.

To see how I think a business plan should be constructed, take a look at DoubleClick's, in the appendix. You may be surprised by how short the plan is. You'll notice a couple of other things as well. We didn't bore anyone with minutiae; and today the company has evolved greatly, but the foundation laid years ago is still clear.

One last point before we start constructing a mythical business plan to give you an example of how all this comes together.

When I am thinking about investing in a company, I use its business plan as an IQ test for the management that wants my money. I am looking to see:

- Are the people who constructed the plan smart enough to figure out exactly what problem they are trying to solve? (I have read many business plans in which, I swear, senior management can't articulate what they are trying to do.)
- Have they anticipated all the significant obstacles that will keep them from doing so? (Most focus only on the obvious or assume no obstacles.)
- Have they realistically projected two or three years out? (I am not so much interested in how big they think the market will be as much as their identification of a rapidly growing market. I'm also looking to see if they're realistic in their approach. There was a famous company many years ago called Power Agent, which predicted it would become the biggest and most profitable company in history during its first couple of years. I was highly skeptical: Why? For one thing, I never could figure out what it planned to do. It seemed to be promising something for everyone, although it was doing something with target marketing. It is out of business.)
- Have they given consideration to something that today is not even a blip on the radar screen (or a dot on the horizon), which could cause them all kinds of problems in the future? If you've given consideration to what might happen, you won't be blindsided. You will be at least mentally prepared for it.

If, after reading the business plan, you can't answer yes to all four of these questions, then you probably don't want to be involved with that company in any form—investor, manager, or employee.

But even if the answers to all the questions are yes, I'm still not done. To find out if I want to be involved, I always examine the plan in detail, looking to see how management handles everything from the executive summary to what marketing people refer to as the five P's: positioning, product, promotion, pricing, and placement.

> People are delusional. They think if they write something down, they have eliminated the problem, so most business plans go on forever. That's a waste of everyone's time. A great business plan can be just ten pages long. As always, it is all about focus.

LET'S CREATE A COMPANY

How might this all play in practice? Why don't we create a mythical company to find out?

Let's say as a result of BPTing needs and BPTing technology, you have decided to create Exercise Excitement, Inc., whose positioning is "Finally, fitness can be fun." (Of course, you could also be establishing Exercise Excitement as a new division of an established company. The process would work the same.)

You have concluded that consumer trends—an aging population who has more money than ever before—coupled with technology and advances in virtual-reality simulations, have made it possible to create exercise equipment that people will want to use. Your business plan explains how you'll turn this concept into reality.

The final form will look like this:

Executive Summary
Market overview

Positioning
Product
Promotion
Pricing
Placement
Competition
Risk
Management
Financials

Now let's see how it all comes together.

BY THE NUMBERS

The first step in creating your business is to write an executive summary. In no more than a page, explain what you have. It will not only crystallize your thinking—keeping it short will keep you focused—it will also convey to everyone what you are going to do, why you will be successful, and why they should want to be part of what you are creating.

Since the summary is the first thing investors and potential employees look at, it needs to be incredibly sexy. If you don't hook people here, you are sunk. They won't read on, and they won't sign on, as either investor or employee. That's why you have to wow them immediately.

But it can't be all flash and glitter. You need to get across three things:

1. What problem you are really solving
2. How big a problem it is
3. Why you are the best company to solve it

Here's what it might look like for our mythical firm:

Exercise Excitement's Executive Summary

Finally, fitness can be fun.

Let's face it, the primary reason most people don't get enough exercise isn't because they are lazy. (It's a factor, but not the primary one.) It's not because they don't have the time. (It's an excuse, not the underlying reason.) And it has absolutely nothing to do with the cost involved. (You could take long walks for free.)

The reason is simply this: Exercise is boring.

Who wants to do the same exercise day in and day out? Even if you watch television while you jog on your treadmill, or listen to CDs while you lift weights, boredom soon sets in. And the interactive exercise equipment out there, with which you row against a stick figure in a boat, won't hold your attention for long.

We live in a GameBoy world, and the best exercise equipment out there is no better than Pong, the Ping-Pong computer game created thirty years ago.

It just isn't appealing to our market. It is a huge market indeed:

- Some forty million Americans are overweight.
- Another ten million who don't have a weight problem say they would like to be in better shape.
- They tell us they are willing to spend an aggregate of $6 billion to improve their health and appearance.

They need a real enticement. We can provide it. By combining state-of the-art animation techniques with the latest in exercise technology we have . . .

You get the idea. As I said, the summary is the most important part of the plan, whether you're starting a business or creating within an established organization. Take your time with it. If you want to use BPT to help create it, you can. In fact, you probably should.

Here's another approach: Do the Executive Summary last, pull the best elements out of the plan, and summarize them up front.

In constructing the plan from scratch, I'd begin by talking in detail about the market you'll address. In the market overview section, you will want to talk about:

- What is the market need?
- Potential market size (in dollars)

- Whether there is existing competition
- How fast the market could grow

Externally, people want to know these things, but even more important, identifying and concentrating on key market drivers will force you to focus. It wouldn't make sense for Exercise Excitement, Inc., to target people making under $50,000 a year. The machines, by definition, will be relatively expensive.

Creating your business plan, your strategy, is an exercise in focus. Nowhere is that more clear than in the central part of the plan, where you discuss the five P's—positioning, product, promotion, pricing, and placement.

POSITIONING

This could be the most important of the P's. In fact, it is so important that when I am constructing a business plan, I usually leave it for next to last. (The Executive Summary is the last thing I do.) By the time we've worked out exactly what we want to say about the other four P's—promotion, pricing, product, and placement—the positioning has become clear. Indeed, every decision you make in creating your strategy helps to shape your positioning.

With positioning, you are trying to tell the world what you stand for. Every business stands for something in a customer's mind. If you don't define your position, what you stand for, somebody else will—and probably not to your advantage.

I have a theory: If you can't explain in a single sentence what your company/product/service does (or will do), then nobody will understand what you have. In other words, if they don't get your positioning quickly, they won't get it at all. You won't have the time to explain it to them, and no one will take the time to figure it out.

We live in a busy world. The average person sees thousands of advertisements in one form or another every day. Venture capitalists get dozens of business plans every day. People don't have the time to sit down and listen to an hour-long spiel about your company. They don't have a half hour to give you. They won't give you even five minutes. People have limited shelf space in their brains and precious little free time in their schedules. You must be able to tell them what you have in a sentence. For DoubleClick, the one sentence was "DoubleClick delivers the most highly targeted advertising on the Internet." For eBay, it might have been "We help consumers sell things to each other in an auction environment." You can always go further if the potential customer is willing to give you the time. But you need to reduce your positioning to a sentence, just in case she isn't willing to spend the time—and she probably won't be.

Entrepreneurs fall in love with their ideas. And they should. They are devoting their lives to them. But it is naive to expect everyone else on the planet to share your enthusiasm. They aren't going to care. As a father, I came to realize that not everyone wanted to see all the baby pictures I had taken. People have their own projects and agendas (and kids). That's why you need to tell them what you have in a sentence. This single sentence is what you say to your employees, customers, suppliers, investors, and everyone you meet at a party. It is who you are.

It's easy to fill a page with what your product or service does; it's far tougher to put it into a coherent, *basic* sentence. How basic? Think "subject + verb + object." That basic. That focused.

(By all means, avoid buzzwords like the plague.)

Is this hard? You bet. But you have no choice, as I learned when I was trying to explain DoubleClick. The business was so complicated that I wanted to explain every bit of it, how the technology worked, why our targeting and people were better, so that people would truly understand what we had. But after watching their eyes glaze over at my first few presentations, I realized that approach wouldn't work. People weren't willing to listen to all that from me, and they won't be willing to listen to all that from you, either in person or in your business plan. Give them the sizzle up front. If you can't get them to read beyond the executive summary, you are doomed.

I like the idea of reducing your idea to one sentence because it forces you to really focus hard, and focus is key for any start-up.

After you get that one sentence down, you can expand on it a bit. When you do, go on the offensive. Tell people what you will do and how you will do it, as opposed to defining yourself against the other guy. So, you would say, "We will be the leading provider of financial information," as opposed to saying, "We will be *The Wall Street Journal* done right." Unless you're going after a very targeted market, you don't want to position yourself in direct opposition to someone else; you will be limiting how big your company can become.

Take the computer industry. Apple has defined itself as the alternative to Microsoft-based personal computers powered by Intel, and that's fine. There will always be a market for people who want to be different, who don't want to go with the market leader.

But as the Apple example shows, those markets tend not to be huge. If you define yourself as an alternative to something else, you are almost always conceding that you will never be the market leader. You are—by definition—limiting how big your organization can grow. The old ad campaign "Avis—we try harder" was catchy, but it also placed Avis second to Hertz.

The better approach is to define your company as the market leader, no matter how small that market is. In the case of our mythical company, it might be "the leading maker of fun, interactive exercise equipment." If you are starting an office-supply firm, the positioning might be "We are the number-one seller of office equipment on Main Street." You can always expand from there. (Always use definitive expressions such as "We will be" as opposed to wishful ones like "We hope to be.")

How do you determine that positioning? Through BPT, of course.

Anytime you are trying to identify and select from a wide number of options, BPT is the way to go.

Once you have determined your positioning, you need to use it constantly and clearly. Put "We are the number-one seller of office equipment on Main Street" on your business cards, stationery, promotional materials, e-mail signature line, etc. Make sure you feature it on the cover of your business plan.

And repeat the message every chance you get. People think saying the same thing over and over again will seem repetitive and boring. But if you do repeat the message, the only person you end up boring is yourself (and that's okay). In talking about how you communicate a company's vision—which, when you think about it, is just another word for its positioning—GE's Jack Welch said, "You have to repeat the same damn speech too many times." And you do. Your message won't sink in the first, second, third, or maybe not even the tenth time, whether you are speaking to your customers or your employees. People are bombarded by too many messages all the time for you to expect yours to break through on the first try.

That's one reason you have to keep repeating it. Here's another. It's easy to think that your audience knows more about your company than it does. If you believe that, when you reiterate your positioning, you feel like you're being repetitious, when, in reality, they probably haven't heard all that you have to say. That's true even when you're talking to employees.

Two last points about this.

First, you are the message. I can't tell you the number of times I've heard people starting a new company say, "And, of course, we will do some consulting work until we are fully under way." Invariably, they end up creating a two-bit consulting firm. If you are committed to something, you have to do it. If people see you splitting your time between two or more ideas, they'll get confused about exactly what you're trying to do. Not surprisingly, they won't take the time to figure it out.

It's no different if you're trying to start something inside an established firm. If you're splitting your time between the new venture and your regular job, odds are you won't be able to do either well. Either you are starting something new or you're not.

Second, as your company gets bigger and bigger and bigger, you have to continually stay focused. Make sure that what your company stands for, what it means in the marketplace—its position—doesn't stray. You'll make tough choices about what you want it to be, and what you don't want it to be. While this is difficult, it is a good problem to have, because it means you've been successful. Once you are a market leader, as defined by your positioning statement, you can enlarge your mission. Until then: Focus.

Now let's quickly run through the other P's. I want to highlight some areas for you to think about and point out a couple of things that have or haven't worked for me over the years.

PRODUCT

What do you have? Why do people need it?

The product-discussion portion of your business plan needs to answer both these questions.

Again, use BPT to home in on exactly what kind of product to create. Suppose your company, Exercise Excitement, Inc., has decided to create an exercise bike that allows users to "compete" in the Tour de France and all the other big bike races. That's great, but you still aren't done as far as the product discussion is concerned. You can use BPT to figure out what specific features your product should have. In the case of Exercise Excitement's interactive bike, that means: Are there goggles? Special shoes? Headphones? Shock absorbers on the bike? Hydraulics to allow the bike to move up and down and side to side? In short, what features will you offer? Use BPT to pin them down.

And when you actually produce your product, it should look a whole lot like what you agreed to create during BPT.

That is a lot easier said than done. When there are problems with the product—and invariably, there are—they usually happen because people try to overengineer what they're creating. That is a mistake. Your first version of the product should respond to what the market needs, and that's it. You can refine it later. By all means, list possible enhancements—all the things that your market might want—in your business plan, but version one should focus on what potential customers need. People buy what they need.

AT&T learned this the hard way. Do people need a telephone? Yes. Do they need to be able to get online? Most of us do. But they don't need to have their telephone bundled into their cable service. People buy what they need, and corporations or start-ups that don't understand that lose lots of money.

The software industry often doesn't understand that. An old industry joke defining software version numbers underscores the point:

Version 1 = the software the company rushed out the door before they ran out of money.

Version 2 = the software the company had to release to avoid being sued. This version contains all the features promised in Version 1.

Version 3 = the version the company was working on when it went bankrupt.

It's funny—to software people, anyway—because it's true. Coming out with products containing exactly what customers needed wouldn't have led to any jokes, but it would have kept a lot more software companies in business. Remember, your first version of the product has to be pretty good. It doesn't have to be perfect, and it doesn't need to contain every feature—the market will tell you what has to be improved and added—but it has to come close to satisfying a consumer's basic needs completely.

Other Potential Product Problems

There are two other problems you can have with your product. Let's go back to our exercise company to show what they are and how they can come about.

You've just opened your doors. Sales are slower than you would have thought—to be blunt, you are way behind your projections—and one of your few customers has said that he would really like to offer people a line of clothing that can be sold along with your equipment. So you rush off and learn all about the clothing business.

This happens all the time. People are always chasing short-term deals, failing to realize that those deals are taking them away from their core strategy. I used to be as guilty of this as anyone.

We suffered from a lack of product focus at ICC, our first company. At one point, we had more products, something like three hundred, than we did employees, two hundred and fifty. Eighty to 90 percent of our sales came from 5 percent of our products, which is usually the case.

As a result, in most of the companies I've been involved with, we've been tough on sticking to what we set out to do. We remain focused. In the scenario I just described, we would say, "This is our strategy: We want to be the world's largest interactive exercise equipment company, and offering clothes doesn't fit our strategy—today. After we master the exercise business, it might be worth another look, but that's somewhere down the line. For now we won't waste time on it." We'd turn that business away even when times were slow.

I know this is hard, especially when you're struggling at a start-up or within an established firm, when times are lean and you want some immediate gratification. But again, it is a matter of focus.

The other problem is more basic. As you grow bigger, you can forget whom you're trying to reach. You need to focus at all times on your target customer and try to satisfy those needs. If you are dealing with a price-sensitive customer and you introduce a high-end product, you aren't meeting your customer's needs. Sure, you want to increase your margins, and introducing higher-priced items is a way to do so, but if that isn't your core market, you are wasting everybody's time.

PROMOTION

Promotion is really marketing communications. However, if we called it "marketing communications," we'd never remember "the four P's and the MC." So let's stick with the five P's and fiddle with the names.

Promotion is a big topic, and people spend a lot of time in college studying it. Let's deal with some of the more common ways to promote your company, consistent with your strategy.

Advertising

I think the biggest lesson I've learned about marketing communications is that everyone is a consumer. Technology companies, especially business-to-business tech companies, tend to get caught up with "speeds and feeds," how fast the product does something: sends data; prints pages, etc. (the speeds); and offers nifty features (the feeds). Save the speeds and feeds for your technical documentation. Your prospects are busy people, and they don't care about the innards of your product. They care about finding solutions to their problems. That is what your advertising must address.

> Your prospects have emotions. They want to be heroes at their jobs. They want to beat their competition and/or save money. You need to solve their problems and play to their emotions with your advertising. You don't have to tell them how you'll do it in your ads. The only message you need to get across is that you will.

That's the general background. When it comes to the advertising it-self, you have to know all the different options. Where will you adver-tise? What media will you advertise in? Within that medium, which outlets will you use? If print is the way to go, then which publications attract your target audience? If you are advertising on the Internet, which sites attract the kind of customers you want?

Once you know your options, you have to determine how best to reach your target customer. To overstate the point, if my customers hang out at the opera, I want to advertise on the classical-music sta-tions. If my product is aimed at commuters, I'll buy radio ad time dur-ing rush hour. If they drink a lot of beer, then I should sponsor wet-T-shirt contests. Everything you do is about highly focusing your fi-nite resources.

In marketing, it's always better to sharply focus your message on a highly defined audience instead of targeting everybody or leaving it to chance. Advertising, as we found out, does not sell the product; it only builds awareness that helps in trying to sell the product. We learned this the hard way.

We were such idiots about all this when we started ICC right out of school. We were near the completion of our first product, Intercom, which, as I mentioned earlier, was the device that connected PCs to Burroughs mainframes. We were absolutely convinced that every busi-ness needed this product, and all we had to do to ensure sales was to place an ad in the leading trade publication, letting everyone know that their worries were over. We believed in the saying "If you build a better mousetrap, then the world will beat a path to your door."

Our customers must have taken a wrong turn. We took out the ad, then sat around (literally) waiting for the sales to come rolling in. No-body called. Not one single person, and we nearly ran out of money waiting for the phone to ring. Since I haven't checked, I don't know if a watched pot never boils. But I can guarantee you this: Staring at a phone won't make it ring.

When we first started, I thought cool technology would sell. Now I know that selling is what sells.

Finally, we bought a prospect list. Over the next few weeks, we all dialed for dollars (i.e., sales), and we eventually got some. From that day on, I never underestimated the importance of selling. Later, when I was helping ISS get off the ground, I spent the majority of my time selling.

The moral?

Advertising will help open doors, not close deals.

Public Relations

PR has shot up on the radar screen of a lot of companies over the years. At DoubleClick, getting PR was fairly easy. We were part of a bigger trend—the Internet. I'll bet we got more PR than any business-to-business company in history. A lot of that had to do with our being in front on the Internet wave. To a lot of media outlets, we representated what was going on overall. So we were the example everyone wanted to use when it came time to do a story on this new Internet thing. We saw PR as a key part of our strategy.

But one of the problems you have with PR is that the more you raise your visibility, the easier it becomes for someone to take a whack at you. In our case, we got hit on the privacy issue. We were the first company many people thought of regarding Internet companies that handle user information over the Net. Some people were scared of the Big Brother issue. Our technology made it possible to track who was visiting many websites anonymously, and some people were concerned that information might be used incorrectly. People confused the issue by talking about how much data was already available and how it could be misused. The reality was far from the speculation. But since we were the leader, all the attention was on us.

What a great position to be in! You want to be the market leader. The privacy issue did little long-term damage to our brand, and by the time people started writing about privacy, we had a very strong brand. We worked with all the concerned groups, and now we are viewed as an example of how to handle privacy responsibly.

I think PR is a great way to get your idea known, but it is a bit Pollyannaish to think that people will rush out and do a story on what you have simply because you or someone you hire tells them it is a good idea. People think that everyone, especially reporters, wants to hear about their product. They don't.

You are never going to get a story from a press release. Press releases are to let the world know you have something to say (hopefully, it's reasonably important). Press releases are ideal for the Internet age: Figure out the best way to get your announcement into people's online mailboxes—at My Yahoo! or AOL or whatever—and you send it out. But to get a story written about you, you need a hook, something to get a reporter's attention.

A good angle is to take the negative. The media loves negatives. For Flexplay, the angle could be "This product will put existing companies—every movie-rental firm, from your local mom-and-pop's to the national chains—out of business."

The only problem with this approach is that it almost guarantees you will be attacked yourself. Like the Boy Scouts, you need to be prepared. With Flexplay, the obvious concern is that the product is disposable, so we're prepared to be attacked for causing landfill problems. We've done studies that show the energy you save by not returning a video more than offsets whatever energy is lost on a product that is thrown away. You actually help the environment by buying Flexplay DVDs.

Branding

A brand can mean only one thing. It can be positioned in someone's brain as having one meaning. Executives tend to overextend their brands. That rarely works out well. It turns out that not many people wanted a Black & Decker coffeemaker, Smucker's pickles, Jack Daniel's beer, or Pepsi Clear (come on, Pepsi is a *cola*!). You want to define the one thing that your company stands for and repeat that message every single time the customer deals with you in any way.

Many companies, especially those that sell directly to consumers—what we now refer to as B2C (business-to-consumer) companies—confuse "brand" with "brand awareness." They think if you can get a lot of people to think of you, you have created a great brand. You haven't. You have created brand awareness. Brand awareness is getting people to recall your name. Branding is about delivering on the promise of the consumer's perception of the product or company.

You can see a good example of the difference if you compare Jack in the Box to McDonald's. Both companies have high brand awareness; that is, most of us have heard of the brands. But with McDonald's, you know without a doubt that you will get the same-quality food, in a timely manner, served in a clean environment, no matter which McDonald's you enter anywhere in the world. What, specifically, can you say about Jack in the Box?

McDonald's has a great brand. The best you can say about Jack in the Box is that it has high brand awareness.

Internet companies spent billions on television advertising to develop brand awareness. However, when consumers went to the sites and bought, they received the wrong product, or the toys showed up after Christmas, or they were billed incorrectly. The companies who spent all that money getting their name known didn't deliver on the promise of their brand. Building a great brand has little to do with advertising. It's about delivering quality products and services over and over again. Your brand is determined by how much customers trust your company.

> In general, the technology market has always put a very, very low value on brand. That has been a mistake, because everyone—even if they are computer geeks—is a consumer. Branding is extremely important whether you are running a B2C company or a B2B company.

Now we can debate whether your company name really matters. If you are selling B2B, the name is less important. Founders often want a name that means something, that refers to what you are selling. I don't think that matters. What does Cisco mean? Double-Click supposedly means something, but no one remembers what it means. It's a catchy name. But the name itself isn't so important. It's the brand.

And the brand flows directly out of how you position your company. You have a lot of choices when it comes to promoting your product. Use BPT to identify all your options, then quickly focus on a few of the options. Concentrate your promotion dollars on these options.

PRICING

You have a lot of control over what you charge, depending on what you're selling. If you're offering something that people can get elsewhere, then you're no different from a farmer with an ear of corn to sell. You have a commodity, and you will get for your product whatever the price is for the commodity at that moment. The corn market, not you, will set your price.

Obviously, you don't want to be a commodity. Oracle and Sun offer critical hardware that most companies need, so they get to charge a premium. If you make floppy disks, you're the same as anyone else who makes floppies, so you can charge only the going rate for floppies. (I might be dating myself here. I'm not sure you can even buy 5 1/4-inch floppy disks anymore.)

At ISS, we deliberately positioned ourselves as a premium product. There was a public-domain version of security scanning software available for free called Satan. Our belief was that large organizations, especially financial institutions, would need a zero tolerance for security breaches and would be willing to pay a premium price for a premium product that scanned for all security issues. We weren't selling on the basis of our individual features. Rather, we concentrated on the fact that it takes only one security hole to jeopardize all the information stored within an organization's computers.

Companies such as Oracle, Sun, and ISS are relatively rare. In most cases, the market will help you determine your pricing. But that doesn't mean you throw your product out there and take whatever results. There were countless Internet service providers who figured they would accept what the market would pay them—nothing—for their service, and they'd make up the difference with advertising revenue. They were wrong. The ad revenue never made up for the shortfall, and they are now out of business.

Break It Down

Wherever possible, try to segment the market, maximizing what you can get in each segment. Airlines are the best example of how segmenting works. All the coach seats on flight 123 from New York to Los Angeles are exactly the same. Yet because the airlines are so good at segmentation, you can have one person—who bought sixty days in advance and agreed to stay over on Saturday night—paying $200 for seat 18A, while someone who bought at the last minute pays $1,200 for seat 18B. That's maximizing segmentation!

There are two other points I want to make about pricing.

One: It must be simple for the customer to understand. Many

times, people try to capture every last drop of value in the pricing model. That's fine, but you will probably be dealing with a wide spectrum of customers, especially in a business-to-business environment. You could sell to everyone from a two-person shop to companies with thousands of employees. Try to set up a pricing structure that deals with each segment of the market, and you may come up with a model that is virtually impossible to understand. So keep the pricing structure simple. People like to buy things that are easy to understand.

Two: You are in business to stay in business. Your pricing has to reflect what you'll need to keep operating. You have to make money to keep going. The idea of selling at a loss (or even cost) in an attempt to gain market share is simply not a good one. People who sell at a loss, using their investors' money to make up the difference, are counting on raising prices once they have a significant share of the market. That is a dangerous strategy. It is very difficult to get people to pay for something that you have been giving them cheap (or for free).

At both ISS and DoubleClick, we priced our products for the long run, so we'd be able to build successful businesses. In both cases, we had low-price competitors who sold against us on price. It was mighty tempting to lower our prices to not lose a deal, but we remained disciplined. Years later, those low-price competitors are out of business, and their clients are ours.

PLACEMENT

Another word for "sales."

I hate to say "never," but you should never try to sell to everybody. Targeting every living thing *and* every ongoing business entity isn't much of a strategy. Lots of people say they are targeting both, but when you dig a little bit, you find they came to that conclusion because of an inherent inability to make a decision. Their rationale?: "How can we go wrong if we pick everything?" Well, you can be extremely wrong, because you aren't focused, and you'll end up trying to be too many things to too many people and failing. Again, focus.

You have to start with a basic idea and an understanding of whom you're trying to target. The more specific you can be in both cases, the better. For example, many companies say they are going to target the XYZ industry, and that's good. But it would be better to say, "We are going to target only large companies within the XYZ sector." In the case of our exercise equipment company, we might decide to target upscale health clubs instead of going after health clubs of all types.

Once you know what market to target, you need to determine the best way to sell to them. Here, briefly, are a couple of approaches.

Telesales

Most people who run sales organizations or departments come from a traditional face-to-face sales force. They look at telesales as a disgusting part of their profession, something *they* would *never* be a part of.

Maybe it was because of my first experience at ICC, but I am absolutely convinced that you can sell any product or any service—including $1 million software packages—by phone. I am convinced because I've done it.

Still, I understand the skepticism. I haven't been in a single organization where the concept of telesales wasn't controversial. Invariably, and ironically, salespeople are usually the ones most against it.

The two biggest myths about telesales are:

- Customers demand face-to-face interactions.
- Only small-ticket items can be sold over the phone.

In my experience at ICC, ISS, and DoubleClick, we routinely sold products that cost $100,000—and some that were priced over $1 million—on the telephone with no face-to-face contact. It's true. At ICC, we sold hardware and software priced at more than $100,000 over the phone. At DoubleClick, we would make advertising sales with no face-to-face meetings. I know firsthand that myths about telesales are just that—myths.

Typically, a company will have several thousand prospects dispersed over a wide area, perhaps even nationwide. It might make sense to establish a physical presence in only five or ten of the top geographic regions. Telesales is a great way to reach the rest of the market. It might be profitable to physically call on customers with a potential for $1 million or more in sales. Telesales is a terrific tool to reach smaller customers, many of whom might graduate to being larger ones who can justify the cost of a salesperson's visit.

The other aspect I love about telesales is that it is highly measurable and scalable. We've always carefully tracked people's progress toward achieving their revenue targets. If you have the money, keep adding telesalespeople until you near saturation of your market. Continuously track key metrics and weed out bottom performers.

The reality is, sales communication and selling are heading this way. People are, for practical reasons, doing very little face-to-face selling. Even supposedly outside salespeople probably spend only 20 percent of their time face-to-face with customers. The other 80 percent of their business is done over the telephone or by e-mail. Of course, building relationships can be key, so maybe you have to visit your biggest accounts. But most of your customers, especially your small- and medium-sized customers, will get much better service over the telephone than they will if you see them sporadically. You can profitably meet only a finite number of prospects (say, five hundred to a thousand), or you might be limited in the number of geographic territories you can cover. With telesales, you don't have these limits.

Joint Ventures and Strategic Partnerships

To me, joint ventures are a lot like going global. I wouldn't worry about it initially.

Joint ventures and strategic business partnerships seem to be very popular, but they rarely work. People think they will have a high degree of success with joint ventures because they seem to make sense. The company you team with brings their strengths to the deal, you bring yours, and armed with more firepower than either of you could come up with alone, you go after the market.

It makes for a great press release. The problem is that both sides usually contribute third-rate people to the venture, and nothing happens.

Joint ventures generally fail because they aren't core to either company. If the idea is really core, you do it yourself. When something isn't strategic, you tend not to focus on it.

Our experience has been decidedly mixed. Our joint venture for DoubleClick Japan is going very well and is now a public company there. Our joint ventures in Spain and Italy did not go so well because our joint-venture partners had a diverse opinion on how the company should be run and funded.

> Do joint ventures for only two reasons: You have a potential partner in a territory that is not strategically critical for your company; or it's the one way to penetrate a territory due to money or tradition (e.g., Japan).

Strategic partnerships are something else I would stay away from. I know they're in vogue, especially among tech-based firms. It seems every company has someone in charge of business development, so their company can form partnerships that make them appear bigger and allow them to move faster than they could otherwise. But I find the whole strategic relationship thing kind of bogus.

I tend to look at business development differently than most people. I figure you already have a sales force selling in a well-structured manner. Given that, business-development people should go out and look for deals that are a bit more integrated. Maybe they sell multiple products together. Or private-label what you have.

The way it is typically done doesn't make sense. Is there any money exchanging hands? If there were, that would strike me as a real strategic relationship.

Going global is one more task I wouldn't spend my time on in the start-up mode. You should be doing everything you can to dominate your local market. When we first started DoubleClick, we had people coming to us and saying, "We want to joint-venture with you and help take you international." We kept saying, "Let us make our mistakes on a small scale. Let us localize what we are doing wrong."

Two other thoughts:

Determine early on if you want to sell direct—that is, through your own sales force. That could include inbound and outbound telemarketers selling exclusively through reps and/or distributors, or some combination of both. You know the advantages, so I won't belabor them: If you use your own people, you control everything and have higher margins. The disadvantages are equally clear: You can grow only as fast as your ability to take on new people. For what it is worth, I think you should outsource the things that aren't core to your business, if you can find someone who can do them faster and cheaper. Companies that focus on a single thing will always do it better than you. At ICC, we outsourced all manufacturing. At DCA, we did not, and it eventually became a big problem: We spent much more time than we should have trying to master something that wasn't one of our strengths. What we learned was that you always do what you do best, and outsource everything else.

At ISS and DoubleClick, we focused all development resources on our core products and bought commercial software whenever possible. Many Internet companies developed all their own software, which eventually killed them (they ended up with mediocre products that had a huge cost structure).

Related to this is the whole question of going OEM–being the private-label supplier to an original equipment manufacturer. You make the stuff, and they stick their name on it. At ICC, we did an OEM deal with Unisys, and they put their name on the products.

While appealing, this is a dangerous road to go down. The good news? You are assured of sales, and your cost of goods sold will be minimal. The bad news? If your OEM customer accounts for the majority–or even a significant amount–of your business, you'll be in serious trouble if they end the relationship. The question is: How many eggs are you willing to put in one basket? In most OEM relationships, nobody knows it was your product to begin with. That makes leveraging what you have difficult.

The last thing I want to say about sales is once you are under way, put a system in place to track wins and losses. Obviously, you want to track whom you talked to and which accounts you won. But it's even more important to track whom you lost to and why you didn't get the sale. There is nothing more insightful than figuring out why you're losing to a competitor.

You will lose deals, so losing one or two shouldn't be the end of the world. Besides, you might lose one deal on price and win the next at a higher price, so you're better off losing the low-margin deal. What you really want to know is whether you're gaining or losing market share.

You do want to pay lots of attention to why you lost a deal. And that can be hard. People want only good news. The great organizations spend a lot of time on their losses. It is fine to celebrate the wins, but it's more important to figure out why you lost when you do.

Analyze lost sales to discover if the issue of why you lost is:

1. Competitive product (could be sales strategy, price, features)
2. Salesperson performance

Most important, you are looking for trends. For example, if you see that Competitor A won 5 percent of the time in the first quarter of the year, 10 percent in the second quarter, and 20 percent in the third, you have a serious problem. To discover why, you need to interview the client as to why you lost the deal. If it's a missing feature, you add it. If it's a bad salesperson, you change him.

> It's great to celebrate wins, but always figure out why you lost a sale. Do you have to change people? Systems? Product offerings? A lost sale ultimately can be beneficial if you learn from it.

Again, you have many options on how to sell your product. Use BPT to identify these options, then narrow them down to the few you will pursue. Focus your sales efforts.

THE OTHER PARTS OF YOUR PLAN

Just because you've completed the P's doesn't mean you're done. You need to address the competition, the risks your management faces, and financials. Each of these variables gives you a chance to focus your business further. Again, the DoubleClick business plan in the appendix will show you in detail how you could deal with each of these factors, but let's touch on each of them now, starting with your competition.

Even if what you are creating is completely new, writing in your business plan "we have no competition" is going to send up red flags. If you don't think you have any competitors, there are only four possible explanations:

- You are arrogant.
- You are stupid.
- You are committing a fraud: You don't really have a product, you are just trying to scam money from investors.
- You have created a product that no one wants.

Assuming you have a product that somebody could want, you have competitors, or you soon will. Everyone—investors, employees, suppliers, your weekly newspaper—will want to know what your plans are for dealing with the present and future competition. You have to talk about not only your main competitors, but also about the companies that could nibble at the edges of your market. OpenMind, our groupware product that allowed numerous people to work on a document at the same time, is the clearest example. We didn't anticipate Microsoft confusing the market with an unreleased product called Exchange. The rumors were that Exchange would do everything that Lotus Notes and OpenMind could do, and lots more, so our sales basically stopped as the market waited for Microsoft's product, which turned out to be not much more than e-mail software.

So, you have to address everything. When you do, you'll be further refining your position in the marketplace.

> A lot of people make the mistake of focusing on the competition as the enemy. It isn't. It is figuring out how to get people to buy from you. Too many people spend too much time trying to figure out how they can destroy their enemy, and not enough on how they can win over the customer.

Risks

For strictly legal reasons, if you know of a risk your company faces, you have to disclose it. Simply listing everything you can think of will probably get you off the hook legally, should you be sued.

But writing "The world might explode," or, in the case of our mythical exercise company, "People could physically evolve past the point where they have arms and legs," doesn't help you from a strategic sense.

A better approach is to use BPT to identify the three key strategic risks. The size of a risk is defined by the probability and size of the negative outcome.

When you apply BPT to the business plan for our exercise equipment company, you may find two potential problems: You might have decided on the wrong type of equipment to offer first (people may be sick of bikes and rowing machines), and your decision to focus on upscale health clubs might be a mistake. But you might find a surprise. It could turn out that the biggest risk your company faces is the fact that the equipment will break. It will get heavy use and little maintenance.

Discovering that risk could force you to:

- Reevaluate the design. Maybe you want to increase the bike's technological components and decrease the mechanical ones in an attempt to limit the potential maintenance problems.
- Bundle in a service contract.
- Sell only through local distributors who can service the equipment on a regular basis.

Your Management Team

People want to know who will be running the company. In the process of telling them, you have a chance to make sure you have the right people in place to implement your strategy. For example, at Exercise Excitement, Inc., clearly you will need a head of manufacturing, along with someone who understands the health-club market. In your business plan, give a very (very) brief bio of all senior management.

Financials

Even though your material must be straightforward, you have a huge opportunity to use this discussion to craft your strategy.

At its most basic, the information you have to provide can be reduced to a fundamental business formula: Revenues minus expenses equals profit.

But in the discussion of revenues, you have the chance to think about how big your addressable market is, how long it will take you to reach it, and when you believe it will saturate. This discussion reminds you that markets tend to develop slower than most people expect, but they ultimately grow larger than projections.

On the expense side, you'll think about how you need to staff the company and, in the case of our exercise equipment company, how you want to handle manufacturing. Do you produce everything yourself? Outsource? Some combination? It always allows you to consider a fact that many companies fail to understand: Pricing is not about what it takes for you to make a profit; it is about what the market is willing to pay.

PUTTING IT TOGETHER

The nice thing about going through this exercise—addressing the five P's and everything else—is that by the time you are finished, you have created the heart of your business plan.

As you will see in the DoubleClick business plan (in the appendix), a summarized discussion about position, product, promotion, pricing, placement, and competition makes up the bulk of the plan. Those factors should be bracketed by a discussion of your competition, risk, management, and finances at the back end, and an executive summary at the front.

AN OPEN BOOK

A quick aside before we sum up: Every employee should have access to the business plan. If you truly want to push decision making down the line, then people need to know where they fit in. The business plan can go a long way toward helping them understand.

At DoubleClick, we put everyone we hire—be it a receptionist in Germany or a corporate CFO in New York—through a week of basic training designed to help them understand the fundamental strategy of our company. If you are an employee, you must understand what we do. And you must understand our strategy—what road we will travel down—and appreciate what role you'll perform. Our business strategy is the central part of that week of training.

I actually had this idea in high school. I hated history. I mean I really hated history. It seemed that all we did was memorize a series of random dates. But I finally had one history teacher who didn't do that. He spent his time on why things happened, not when. To him, understanding the underlying causes of the Civil War was more important than the fact that it occurred between 1861 and 1865. I really appreciated that approach. For the first time, I could learn some history.

I carried the idea of putting things into context when I went into business. I wanted to make sure people understand why we do things the way we do. Yes, they need to understand our costs and their specific job responsibilities, but the context and framework of the decisions that we make are most important. That's where the weeklong orientation fits in. Most people appreciate knowing what the organization is trying to accomplish and where they fit in.

It's all part of the strategy.

SUMMARY

1. **Use BPT to identify all options and focus on a few.** Strategy is nothing more than focusing on a few things and ignoring everything else. Your business plan is a reflection of that. Focus, focus, focus. This is the place where you show the world what you are going to do and, perhaps more important, what you are not going to do.

2. **Tell everyone how you are going to do it.** In your business plan, show people how you will turn your idea into a reality.

3. **Remember, this is a selling document.** You don't have to hype—in fact, you shouldn't—but you do have to entice. If you haven't hooked them by the time they finish the executive summary, odds are, they won't keep reading.

4. Your business plan should follow the following outline:

Executive Summary
Market overview
Positioning
Product
Promotion
Pricing
Placement
Competition
Risk
Management
Financials

CHAPTER

GETTING (AND KEEPING)
THE MONEY

For a small piece of paper, it carries a lot of weight.
—"For the Love of Money," THE O'JAYS

or

Money is the root of all evil,
and a man's got to have his roots.
—UNKNOWN

There is a great paradox that surrounds getting the necessary funds to turn your idea into reality. When you don't need the money, everyone wants to give you some, and when you really need it, nobody will give you any.

The solution to this paradox: Never put yourself in the position where you need money. (Or at least don't show people how desperate you really are.)

The problem, of course, is that very few of us find ourselves starting a company with all the financing we need, or are given an unlimited budget to create something within an established corporation. Since that is the case, let's talk about how you can come up with the money to make your idea a reality.

GETTING MONEY WITHIN AN ESTABLISHED FIRM

Unlike start-ups, where the process is pretty much the same in every instance, getting money within a company differs radically from company to company. For that reason, I'm going to be a bit broad here, but let me discuss the two most likely scenarios: You want to extend an existing product line, or you want to enter a new market.

In either case, you will be competing for that money with your colleagues. Somebody will win (they'll get the funding) and somebody will lose (they'll go unfunded).

Most large organizations have a fixed method for reviewing and funding projects. They'll likely employ something called internal rate of return (IRR) or net present value (NPV). Explaining how to calculate either of these formulas is way beyond the scope of this book or my own skills.

Essentially, somebody in the company manufactures the anticipated return on the money invested. Whichever projects can promise to deliver not only the minimal expected return but the *best* returns of all the projects under consideration for funding has the best chance at the money.

In general, I think this approach and these yardsticks are garbage. Sure, for an obvious line extension, you can probably produce some fairly accurate numbers. But for any significant innovation, you are attempting to quantify the unquantifiable. This is why, for start-ups, most venture capitalists (VCs) ignore these types of analysis. In Excel, you can easily monkey with any of the many variables. Variables are nothing more than assumptions.

What can you do if your company uses an internal rate of return to fund projects? You can buy multiple copies of this book and distribute them to the funding committee (there's almost always a committee) and tell them that their approach is garbage because Kevin O'Connor says so. However, you'll lose, because I don't work at McKinsey or have a Harvard MBA (was that redundant?).

Or you can play the game. You better know what the minimal IRR/NPV required is going in. And you better know who you're competing with and how good their Excel skills are.

If you're creating a product that is a logical extension of an existing line, then you're most likely to get funding from that profit center. The challenge is that the money will inevitably come from an older, highly profitable product. Folks in that group won't appreciate funding your new product only to receive none of the benefit.

Anticipate a highly political struggle. Make sure you have support from the senior executives of that group. Otherwise, you either won't get funding or you'll have an ax hanging over your head.

If you're going outside your company's traditional market, then strongly push for the company to treat it like a start-up. Get your own budget, your own dedicated people, your own office space, etc.

That brings us to the problems that start-ups face when they look for funding.

FUNDING A START-UP

If you are starting out, odds are you won't be able to obtain all the funding at once. You'll probably have to go through several stages of raising money, depending on how bold or unsuccessful your plans are.

There are roughly three categories of fund-raising:

- The early stage: raising money from family and friends
- The later stage: Professional investors enter the picture
- Public financing, such as going public

During each step in the process, remember the most important adage there is for getting the money to build your business: Always raise two to three times the money you think you need.

There are two interrelated reasons why entrepreneurs usually don't do that:

1. They are optimistic.
2. They are greedy.

Because they are optimistic, people starting companies tend to raise the minimum amount of money, convinced that they will always be able to go out again when their company is more valuable. (They figure they can get investors to pay more for a smaller piece of their firm.)

That brings us to the second reason why they don't raise enough money: Entrepreneurs never want to part with any of their equity. They rarely bring in outside investors willingly.

The problem with both traits is obvious, but always forgotten. If you put off going back for more money, you may find the capital markets closed when you desperately need them to be open. And if you start hoarding equity—instead of selling part of your company to outside investors when it is time to do so—you will never be able to grow your business. Or worse, you'll try to raise money when you desperately need it, and people won't give it to you when you need it.

To avoid these problems, let me suggest you keep this simple formula in mind: 100 percent $\times$ \$0 = \$0

In other words: It doesn't matter how much stock you have in a valueless company. You want your company to be worth something, and the only way that is going to happen is if:

1. You bring in outside investors who can help it grow.
2. You bring them in early.

There are two other reasons for doing so. No business plan in the world can anticipate all the problems you will face. It's not a question of *if* you will face problems. The only questions are when and how bad those problems will be. When the bad times hit, you will want money readily available in your corporate checking account. On a more pleasant note, you might encounter unique opportunities that require capital now rather than later. In either case, you will want money on hand.

I can't begin to tell you all the sob stories about Internet companies that ran out of cash in 2000 and 2001 when the capital markets suddenly closed. For the previous couple of years, any Internet company got funded when it wanted and at the levels it wanted. As a result, the people who started those companies thought money would always be easy to come by. So they would raise a little money each time they needed some, certain that their valuation would continue to climb and they would give away a smaller piece of the company when it came time to raise more.

They learned the hard way that this kind of trend does not continue indefinitely. And when the trend turns, it drops off the cliff. Adam Smith may have said capital markets are rational. He was wrong.

As I write this, the capital markets are shut as tight as a drum. Companies are trading below their cash value. We've gone from $1 billion of valuation for companies with no business model to a market where a dollar isn't even valued at a dollar. Never, ever assume that markets are rational, and plan your money raising accordingly.

Capital markets open and close. They'll invariably be closed when you need money the most, and you'll never know when they will open again. Always raise money when you don't need it. We went public at DoubleClick relatively early for that very reason. We had been in business under four years, but people wanted to take us public in 1998. It was the right decision. The money was available.

When you have no money, you're desperate, and people can smell it. People hate desperate people and either don't fund them or charge an awful lot for the money.

When people are willing to give you money, take it. Don't worry about how much of an equity stake you'll have after you sell off shares. Remember our formula: 100 percent $\times$ $0 = $0. You aren't selling off everything you own, and if you are successful, any stake you own is bound to be worth a lot of money. The only thing you should care about is whether the value of every share increases or decreases every time you raise money.

Early Stages of Funding

In the perfect situation, you use other people's money to turn your idea into reality. You keep most of the equity in the company, you incur no personal financial risks, and you draw a healthy salary.

That's the perfect situation, but it isn't usually the reality. The reality is that once you've developed an idea (see chapters 2 and 3), you need someone to fund it, and at least initially, that someone will be you and the other founders (if there are any).

You have to put up as much money as possible. If you are young and starting out, that probably means risking everything (which won't be much). If you are in your thirties or forties, with a couple of kids and a mortgage payment, no one will expect you to jeopardize everything you own, and you would be an idiot to do so. In fact, I wouldn't invest in your company if you did. It would show a lack of judgment.

Part of the reason investors won't ask people with families to risk all their assets is simple human decency, but that's only part of the explanation. There is a business reason as well. You don't want the founders putting everything on the line, because it can paralyze their management skills. Every time they have to make a decision, they'll wonder whether the wrong move is going to cost them their house and their kids' ability to go to college.

Even though I don't expect them to pledge everything they own, I do expect them to have a lot of skin in the game, if I am going to invest in their company. That means you'll have to put up what is a significant amount of money for you. If you aren't willing to invest your own money in what you are doing, how can you expect anybody else to invest theirs?

In addition, the founders can't take much money out of the business in its early days. If they do, investors will take it as a vote of no confidence. So you need to work for free, or almost for free, initially. During my first year at ICC, I made $6,000, which put me below poverty level. (That was okay. I was committed to what we had, and besides, all you need to stay alive are bean burritos and beer.)

Here is the thing to remember about all this: Investors and founders are like a ham-and-egg breakfast. The chickens (investors) participate, but the pig (you) is committed.

This situation doesn't last forever. Once a firm is growing and doing well, the investors will sometimes urge the founders to take some of their money off the table. That way, the founders will get at least a decent return on their investment; it will also take some of the pressure off them (they're still running the company at this point) so they can make better decisions about the business. But that is a ways down the line. In the early days, you are going to be strapped. Accept that as a fact going in.

Nothing is more frustrating than having a great idea but no business history to inspire traditional investors. If that describes your situation, your initial funding will come from you, your family, and your friends.

That's What Friends Are For

After you have exhausted your own resources, you turn to your friends and relatives. Ideally, you have a lot of friends with money, you come from a wealthy family, or you have at least one dumb rich aunt you can tap. When we started ICC in 1983, venture capital was virtually unknown in Cincinnati, Ohio. Unfortunately, we didn't come from wealthy families. We ended up getting around $25,000: $12,500 from my parents and $12,500 from the parents of our cofounder, Bill Miller. In those days, you could start a software company with $25,000 from your parents.

Let me stress something about going to family and friends. Never take money from people who can't afford to lose it. It's wrong. Our parents could afford to take a $25,000 bath, though they wouldn't have been happy about it. Fortunately, ICC turned out to be a great investment. My parents' $12,500 turned into stock worth almost $1 million. Mom and Dad were pleased with their decision to back us.

I know the two basic arguments against turning to family and friends: You never want to mix business and pleasure; and if you lose your friends' money, they won't be your friends.

That all sounds reasonable, but desperate times call for desperate measures. When you're starting a company, you're desperate (remember, don't show it). You need money. And if you need money, you'll go to the people you know who have some, and at the beginning, that is probably your family and friends. Besides, if you generate tremendous returns for them, they will definitely like you a lot more. You can't imagine how much they might like you.

> When you ask family and friends for money to help start your company, it should be treated as an investment and not a loan. Anybody who would lend money to a start-up is a real sucker. If you're going to take equity risk, you should get equity returns. If you lend money to a start-up, you are taking equity risk with only loan returns. That's dumb. Investors should insist—and entrepreneurs should readily agree—that the money is for a purchase of stock in the company.

Yes, asking for money is difficult, but you have something going in your favor—other than the fact that investors hopefully find you trustworthy and backable. People like the opportunity that comes with investing in new companies. They hear the stories about family members putting up $10,000 to help company XYZ get started, and that investment is now worth a not-so-small fortune, and they want to get in. If you're really lucky, they might even be offended if you don't ask them to invest.

When you're raising money from investors—even when those investors are your family and friends—you have to give everyone the same terms every time you do a round of financing.

A lot of people believe you should squeeze the last penny out of your investors. I don't feel that way. I have always tried to offer all of our investors very fair deals. My belief is you should try to make your investors a lot of money. I never liked squeezing people. Besides, if you squeeze them, there's not a lot of goodwill to draw on when things go bad, and there invariably will come a point when they do.

Okay. You've found your start-up money. Your company grows. You need more money. Now what?

Finding Angels

Once you have exhausted family and friends as a source of income, you can move on to angels. The massive number of previously success-ful start-ups out there, coupled with the seemingly hundreds of thou-sands of people who have sold successful private companies in recent years, has created an unprecedented number of angel investors. These are private individuals who invest money in fledging businesses in the hopes of getting a greater return than they would from putting that money in the stock market or anywhere else.

Angels can be divided broadly into two categories:

1. Those who are relatively new to the process tend to invest around $25,000.
2. "Professional angels," people who have done a lot of deals, may invest $50,000 to $500,000. Venture capital funds have dramatically increased in size over the years—something we will talk about in a minute—forcing them to invest in later-stage start-ups. "Professional angels," like me, are now performing the job of a classic VC. I'm a PA.

Angels can be great for entrepreneurs, since they have money and experience. Like most smart investors, angels tend to stick to their knit-ting. They invest where they have the most understanding and put their money in ventures where they have a good handle on what goes on. People who made money in retailing tend to invest in retail start-ups. Angels who earned their fortunes, or semifortunes, in technology usually look to back other high-tech companies. That describes me. I get more and more nervous the further I get from my area of expertise. I made the classic mistake of investing in a company (that produced a desk reference about dental drugs) in an industry I knew nothing about at the time (publishing). I lost $40,000. Ironically, in the process, I learned a lot about publishing and advertising, which eventually helped me with DoubleClick. I look at this experience as my $40,000 MBA.

Fortunately, a good percentage of my investments in early-stage companies have had a happier ending. My decision to help fund ScreamingMedia, HotJobs, and ISS are examples of what happens when angel investing works for everyone.

As you'll remember, I couldn't believe my good fortune back in early 1995 when I met Chris Klaus, the founder of ISS. Chris had built a very clever and sophisticated security scanning product that systematically checked for hundreds of security vulnerabilities across the thousands of computers and network devices of a company. Chris was twenty years old when he started the company and had dropped out of Georgia Tech to pursue the idea.

When I met Chris, ISS consisted of he and a Georgia Tech student who was a part-time employee. Still, his company had successfully built its first product, Internet Scanner, and had sold it to about ten major clients for around $25,000 a pop. During due diligence, I interviewed each of those initial clients, and they all loved the product. Even more impressive, Chris had come this far using just his own money (I think he was living in his grandma's apartment at the time to save money). I invested immediately. It worked out very well for both of us.

The problem with angels is that they typically invest as a part-time job, so it can be difficult to get their attention. In fact, it may be hard to find them at all. They aren't as well organized as the venture capitalists, people we will discuss in a minute. In many cities, you can find an informal network of angels who will get together and share ideas. Also, check out Garage.com, a site that brings together entrepreneurs with investors.

In the best of all worlds, you approach angels strategically. Look for those who can give you money *and* advice–they'll serve as de facto boards of directors and advisers. Things don't always work out this well, so at the very least, you want them to give you money.

Could your customers–or potential customers–serve as angels or VCs? It can happen. Sometimes after you've completed your sales presentation, the person on the other side of the table will say, "That sounds really great. We'd love to invest, as well." But most companies aren't set up to invest. From a customer's perspective, watching a sales presentation and then getting hit up for an investment doesn't leave a real warm and fuzzy feeling. If a customer decides to invest, great. But don't count on it happening.

Let me mention one other financing alternative before we move on.

Sometimes potential entrepreneurs try to develop an idea from an "incubator," a work environment typically set up by a university or group of entrepreneurs that supplies support services for fledging companies. Incubators are a flawed business model.

Here's why. My message so far has been: Focus only on the things you need to do to create a successful business. Incubators typically offer things like legal services, accounting, office space, and equipment–none of which is essential to the success of a start-up.

Some incubators believe that an experienced entrepreneur can crank out lots of ideas that magically turn into companies. The theory goes that these people will come up with the ideas, the support staff will take care of everything else, and poof, you have a lot of companies. That isn't the way the real world works.

There needs to be a continuum from idea to established company. Where would you bet your money–on one incubator trying to be a leader in ten markets or on ten separate companies trying to be leaders in those same ten markets? I am not a big fan of incubators. Back in

1995, we considered starting what would have been one of the first in-cubators. I'm glad we worked on developing ISS and DoubleClick instead.

Another version of incubators is the so-called keiretsus, or venture capitalist networks. These are modeled on the failing Japanese keiretsus. Essentially, it's a network of companies that have common investors who (are forced to) do business with one another. This was a very clever financial model back in the days of the "new" economy. It worked then because of the revenue arbitrage. In a soaring market, one dollar of revenue equaled ten dollars of market cap. For example, if you had a network of ten companies doing $1 million of business with each member, that network would be valued at $100 million, even though no real value was created.

In declining or flat stock markets, that model doesn't work. Also, the ownership is in only one direction, and it's unlikely that each member has the best product or service.

Avoid these types of relationships if you have the choice. Your biggest goal during this first round of financing—as you tap family, friends, and angels—is to raise enough money (times two or three) to bring your first version to market and create a customer base you can refer other people to when they consider buying from you or funding you.

> There's a reason why incubators haven't produced many, if any, great companies: They don't work.

Right about now, when I am explaining the process of gaining the money you need to turn your idea into a reality, somebody invariably asks about getting early funding from a bank, either in the form of loans or by drawing on credit lines.

Get a bank loan as soon as you can, but you'll need something to secure first (like equipment or accounts receivable). At this point, you don't have much to offer a bank in the way of security. They will ask you to personally guarantee the loan, something which makes no sense to me. If you have the money in some other form, you might as well put it in your company in the form of equity and not bother paying the bank interest.

You should always have credit lines in place so you can draw on them when you need them. But again, the banks are going to want collateral.

The other general problem with loans is that you have to pay them back or bad things happen. (The banks take over.) If you don't feel like you have a business with sufficient cash flows to pay back the banks' interest, you should sell equity. Just ask the now-bankrupt high-flying company Exodus—they borrowed some $6BB they couldn't pay back. Should have sold equity!

Living on Credit Cards

There is one form of loans that is relatively easy to get: credit cards. If you're young and single and don't have any assets, you might as well run up your credit cards to gain the funding you need. Either the company takes off and you can pay them off, or the company doesn't and the credit card companies took all the risk. (Though that is not as true as it once was, since the new bankruptcy laws allow credit card companies to come after you for many years.)

Back at ICC, we couldn't believe it when American Express gave us a company credit card. An American Express card is an especially good one, since it doesn't have a real credit limit. A week after we got the card, Amex called and asked if the credit card had been stolen.

We said, "No, why do you ask?"

"Well, you've managed to run up a hundred thousand dollars in expenses. Are you sure you can pay?"

Amex eventually received their money—but it was close.

Okay. You've found more money. Your company grows even larger. Now you need even more money.

LATER-STAGE FINANCING

You might end up doing several rounds of financing after you bring your first product to market and before your long-dreamed-of IPO. Typically, as you move to the later stages of financing, you will deal with extremely wealthy investors, strategic investors, or venture capital (VC) firms. They all come with pluses and minuses.

The problem with wealthy investors is the same as with angels: You have to find them. There is no directory of rich people you can turn to and begin dialing for dollars. However, if you were successful in attracting some angels they might be able to make the introductions for you to their wealthier friends.

Getting strategic investors—companies that are your suppliers and/or customers—to invest in you sounds good. Who wouldn't want to have closer ties to firms that can help make you successful?

The problem with taking money from them is fourfold.

First, most companies aren't set up to do investments, so it's a hassle just to create a mechanism to get the money.

Second, you have to worry about whether the strategic investor has ulterior motives, like sucking everything you know out of your brain so he can enter the market himself; cornering you so your firm doesn't become a threat; etc.

Third, investors and your strategic partner's operating people are different and have different agendas. Just because the person doing the investing for your strategic partner promises to do all sorts of things (open channels of distribution, provide contacts) doesn't mean the operating people will actually do it. In fact, they're guaranteed not to do anything if they perceive you to be a competitor or threat.

Finally, other firms within the industry will be reluctant to buy from you, thinking they are helping to fund a competitor.

We experienced that firsthand in the early days of DoubleClick. Our major investor, BJK&E, the parent company of Bozell advertising, was strategic. The investment seemed to make sense to both of us. BJK&E was a large ad-agency holding company, and ad agencies were our clients.

However, we found out that BJK&E competitors didn't want to do business with us. BJK&E recognized the problem and dramatically reduced its position.

This is one of the main problems with strategic investments: You rarely get anything but disadvantage.

And then there are the venture capitalists.

VCs 101

A lot of people hate venture capitalists. Some call them "vulture capitalists." You'll probably find a loser behind those words. I have a huge regard for VCs and think they are largely responsible for the incredible expansion in our economy in the last couple of decades (though, as I write this, we seem to be going though a contraction). The U.S. start-up engine is the envy of the world, and the VCs provide the gas to make this engine run.

VCs have one major goal, and it's to make a lot of money off your company. But that's okay. If they make a lot of money, you will, too, as we will see. Contrary to popular belief, VCs won't do anything to make a buck and generally will do what's best for your company long-term. Just like any other company, a good VC has a reputation to maintain. Success for VCs means more deal flow going forward, so they aren't likely to cut corners at your expense. Doing so will limit the number of deals they see in the future.

Of course, not all VCs are great or ethical. Some are borderline crooks. In fact, I recently had a less-than-positive experience with a VC firm that promised one thing–they were going to hold on to their stock–and did another: They sold it at the first opportunity, hurting the share price and all the other investors. That has been the exception in my dealings with VCs.

That just underscores the need for you to check their references carefully. Also, check with other companies they have funded, even if they aren't given as references.

Make no mistake about it: Greed is what motivates VCs (and most other investors). There's nothing wrong with greed, and, best of all, it's easy to predict. There is no hidden agenda, like you might find with strategic investors.

It's important to understand what VCs are looking for when they evaluate companies. After all, the more you know about what they need, the more you can tailor your presentation accordingly.

While all VCs are different, and have different requirements, they all ask about the following four things:

- Is the target market sufficient to support a public company? That's another way of asking: Could your sales top at least $500 million a year?
- Is your product unique? Does it solve a real problem and have sufficient barriers to keep others from entering the market?
- Does your company have an effective strategy to lead the market?
- What kind of management team do you have?

As you can tell from the questions, VCs aren't interested in building small companies. Let's spend some time going over exactly what they look for.

Their primary goal is to fund a leading company in a large segment of an existing or new market. If they are successful, the company will be well positioned to do an IPO or be bought by a larger, public company. That's the VC's exit strategy, how they plan to get their money back and earn a (substantial) profit.

All of the blue-chip VCs (firms such as Kleiner Perkins, Greylock,

Sigma + Partners, and Bain Capital) have massive amounts of money to invest these days. These firms tend to be relatively small, with few partners. A typical partner can be involved with ten or so companies. The effort it takes to make a small or large investment is roughly the same, so VCs can afford to make only large investments, typically from $5 million to $100 million.

As a result, VCs have steadily moved away from early-stage investing; it takes too much time, and they can't earn enough on their investments. This shift has created a huge window of opportunity for angel investors who want to invest $10,000 to $1 million.

If you want to attract VCs, in your business plan you need to identify a sufficiently big market—and it has to be a real market, not just an imagined one—in which you can become a top player. The VCs will want to know if your product solves an actual problem. Cool technology alone isn't going to cut it with the top VCs (though during the Internet craze, all the rules went out the window).

Assuming your product does solve a problem, VCs will ask whether it is unique or has an existing (or looming) competitor. Don't worry: The game isn't over if there are existing solutions. But the bar to funding does get raised. As we have discussed elsewhere, you can't be incrementally better than the established competition; you need to be radically better. Your product needs to be, say, one tenth of the cost of, or perform ten times faster than, the alternative. People will not abandon existing and proven solutions for a new product from a new company unless there is a real strategic advantage to switching.

VCs know that predicting the future with any accuracy is impossible. They also know that many existing assumptions will change rapidly, and as a key part of their decision about whether to fund your company, they'll try to learn whether you have a management team that will not only sense these changes but react to them quickly. That means they will spend a lot of time trying to figure out if you are the right person to lead the company in the years ahead.

Most founders take the role of CEO in the beginning, assuming that since they came up with idea and were the primary force behind it, they are entitled to be CEO for as long as they want. The harsh reality is that many founders are not fit to be CEOs, and most VCs will reserve the right to appoint new ones.

That's understandable, difficult as it is for some founders to accept. The talents and skills required to create and launch a new idea are not the same as those required to build a lasting company. If you are an entrepreneur/founder, this creates a real catch-22. If you balk at the VCs' insistence on appointing the CEO at some future point, they will not have the confidence that you'll step aside should it become necessary, and they won't invest.

Don't take it personally, but you will probably be fired as CEO and asked to take a job within the company that fits more with your talents. That is because of a lesson VCs have learned the hard way: A huge percentage of companies die in their early days simply because the founder is an egomaniac or incompetent.

Ironically, being an egomaniac can be a great attribute when you are trying to pioneer a new market. Indeed, in the early days, it is frequently nothing more than the founder's drive that keeps the company going. But that same maniacal zeal can destroy the company as it starts to get bigger. It keeps you from building a strong team, and it slows the firm's rate of growth, since everything gets funneled through you, the founder.

Founders should always try to hire people smarter than they are, then assume a role for which they are most qualified. It might be head of sales, chief technology officer, or even simply as a board member with no day-to-day responsibilities. ISS is a great example. The founder was twenty years old and a technical genius. He knew technology better than anyone else, but he had never worked at a company, let alone run one. As ISS got bigger, he became chief technology officer, which was the right position for him and the company. Don't confuse your ownership with employment.

One last general point about VCs. As we said, they can make only so many investments, and an investment in your company could last many years. The VC knows she will be working closely with you, and nobody likes to work with a jerk. So if you are a jerk, good luck.

How to Get a VC to Return Your Call

The harsh truth is that thousands of business plans are sent to VCs every year, and there is no way they can read them all. It is extraordinarily rare for an over-the-transom plan to get opened. In other words, if you send an unsolicited business plan to a VC who doesn't know you, it will get filed.

To operate as efficiently as possible, most VC firms create a huge network of talent scouts. These are generally executives of companies that VCs have previously funded—men and women who, after their firms go public, often become limited partners in the VC funds themselves. (Just to put this in context, I am now a member of a half-dozen funds.)

When I come across companies that I think are worth funding, I'll introduce them to the venture capital firms that I've worked with in the past. Even most of these companies don't get funded. It's that tough.

Each VC firm must know fifty people like me, people with some experience who are presumably experts in their fields, have a proven track record, and are looking for potential investment opportunities. Angels are talent scouts as well. This network of talent scouts is one very good reason you should try to bring in some well-placed angel investors early on: They know where to go for the big money, and they bring enormous credibility.

You might think the way the financing world works is unfair, and if you don't know anybody, it is. But I don't know any other way it could work. Ideas are cheap, and there are too many out there to fund.

Besides, this industry isn't really any different from most other industries. How many frustrated musicians are out there playing the bars and clubs, waiting to get their big break? They probably wonder why they can't walk into the offices of Sony and cut a record deal. The reason is simple: If they could, the line would be a mile long, and the folks at Sony wouldn't get anything done. Life isn't fair.

Negotiating the Deal

Okay, you've gotten some VCs to return your calls. Talk to them, but talk to no more than ten. (Focus your efforts.) If you're in the enviable position of turning away VCs, you must have something hot. If you do, most venture capital firms will be begging for appointments. Without question, there is a lemming effect when it comes to investors of all kinds, including VCs—the more people they see lining up to invest, the more they want to invest. If there's no competition, everyone thinks there's something wrong and will run away fast. You always want your VCs believing that they are competing for the deal.

During this phase, never, and I mean *never,* tell the VCs whom you are talking with. This is high-stakes poker. The VC community is a very tight group, and they have in the past—and will again in the future—go in on deals together. If you tell them which other VCs you are talking with, the moment you hang up, they will call their friends at that firm to compare notes. That will ultimately reduce the price they are willing to pay.

On the other hand, VCs are very protective of their deals and don't want other VCs to find out about them. If you don't tell them to whom you're talking, they won't call around for fear of alerting others.

As long as we're talking about things not to do, here's another one. Avoid throwing out valuation numbers when people start discussing what your company is worth. Whatever number you say, you'll get something less, so you don't want to offer up a number that is too low. If you go too high, the VCs will think you are insane and will walk. Avoid addressing the subject directly. Give the VCs a valuation range where the low number is still too high. This will get the VCs thinking big, but will also show you are willing to negotiate.

How do you know how much your company is actually worth? You don't. You go out and get comps—learn what comparable businesses are valued at—but even that's basically worthless at this point, because your company doesn't have much of a track record. The value of your company will ultimately be determined by the supply and demand of investors.

Not too long ago, valuations were ridiculously high. For example, there was a company, Living.com, that an investment bank said was worth $1 billion if it went public. Eight or nine months later, it went bankrupt. That is not the only example from the Internet craze of the late 1990s.

A few years ago, I was involved in a potential acquisition. I had just offered the twenty-six-year-old founder and CEO $82 million for his company, which had very little revenue, wasn't making money, and was only a couple of years old. The young CEO, who would have gotten rich from the deal, told me he was insulted by my offer.

I kept asking him if he had any clue how much money $82 million actually was.

He turned down the deal, went public, and ended up selling the company for just about cash value, which was a tiny fraction of the $82 million I had offered. The moral? Don't fool yourself. Valuations are based on what people are willing to pay at the time, and values change quickly.

When you are raising money, you want to get two or more investors interested in your company so they can bid the value up. You can't hold an auction with one person. Everyone thinks they're getting a deal at an auction, but on average, they end up paying 50 percent over retail.

Next Step: The Term Sheet

Assuming you have meetings with a number of VCs, your next goal is to get the almighty term sheet.

Let me say this up front: I wouldn't care if I got a term sheet from a shylock who placed a one-dollar valuation on my fledging company. It's a term sheet! And a term sheet means that somebody is sufficiently interested in your company to invest. Once you have someone interested, you can set off to create competition and get the price up. That's why the first term sheet is so important.

So what is it?

A term sheet is simply a one-to-three-page document detailing the terms at which an investor is willing to put up money, the amount he will invest, and at what valuation. The lawyers will use this document to draw up all the contracts.

While there is no typical term sheet, here is a representative sample:

SUMMARY OF DRAFT TERMS XYZ CORP.

February 14, 2003

This memorandum summarizes the principal terms of the Series B round venture capital financing of XYZ Corp. (the "Company"). The Company was incorporated in Delaware on _____ ___, 2001.

KEY PROVISIONS

Investors

Security	Units consisting of (a) one share of Series B Convertible Preferred Stock of the Company (the "Series B Preferred Stock") and (b) one warrant exercisable, under certain circumstances, into one share of common stock of the Company.
Price per share	$1.67 per Unit ($1.66 per share of Series B Preferred Stock (the "Original Issue Price") and $0.01 for each Warrant).
Aggregate proceeds	$2.0 million. Minimum proceeds of $1.0 million required for initial closing.
Expected closing date	March 15, 2002. Additional closings may be held at the option of the Company within one hundred twenty days after the initial closing, at times selected by the Company.

TERMS OF SERIES B PREFERRED STOCK

Dividend provisions   Annual 6% per share dividend on the Series B Preferred Stock. Dividends payable if, as and when determined by the Board of Directors ("Board"). Dividends are not cumulative. For any other dividends or distributions, the Series B Preferred Stock participates with Common Stock on an as-converted basis.

Liquidation preference First pay original purchase price plus accrued dividends on each share of Series B Preferred Stock. Thereafter, the holders of Series B Preferred Stock and Common Stock shall share proceeds on a pro rata (as converted) basis until the holders of Series B Preferred Stock have received two times their cost. Thereafter, balance of proceeds paid to Common Stock.

A consolidation or merger of the Company or sale of all or substantially all of its assets shall not be deemed to be a liquidation or winding up for purposes of the liquidation preference but instead appropriate provision shall be made to carry forward the rights, preferences and privileges of the Series B Preferred Stock in any successor corporation, provided that the holders of at least 51% of the then outstanding shares of Series B Preferred Stock may waive such treatment by written consent.

Redemption   The Series B Preferred Stock shall not be redeemable.

Conversion   Convertible at any time at option of holder into one share of Common Stock (subject to anti-dilution adjustments).

Automatic conversion The Series B Preferred Stock shall be automatically converted into Common Stock, at the then applicable conversion price, (i) in the event of an underwritten public offering of shares of the Common Stock at a public offering price per share that is not less than three times the Purchase Price and an aggregate offering price of $7,500,000 (a "Qualifying IPO") or (ii) the date upon which the Company obtains the vote or consent of at least 51% of the then outstanding shares of Series B Preferred Stock to such conversion.

Anti-dilution provision The Series B Preferred Stock shall be entitled to proportional anti-dilution protection for stock splits, stock dividends, etc. Additionally, the conversion ratio shall be adjusted on a broad-based weighted average basis in the event of a future dilutive issuance (an issuance of equity securities of the Company at a pre-money valuation less than $5 million). A dilutive issuance shall not include the sale of Common Stock reserved for employees, consultants and the like or shares issued pursuant to partnering arrangements, lease lines or other standard exceptions. Proportional adjustments for stock splits and dividends.

Warrants

The Company shall issue to each investor one Warrant along with every share of Series B Preferred Stock purchased by such investor.

If the Company does not consummate an equity financing with a pre-money valuation of the Company greater than the sum of (x) the proceeds of this Series B financing and (y) $5,000,000 by May 31, 2003, the Warrants shall be exercisable by the holder of such Warrant (the "Warrant Holder") into a number of shares of Company common stock equal to fifteen percent of the number of shares of common stock into which the Series B Preferred Stock, held by such Warrant Holder, is convertible, calculated as of the closing of this Series B financing.

If the Company does not consummate an equity financing with a pre-money valuation of the Company greater than the sum of (x) the proceeds of this Series B financing and (y) $5,000,000 by May 31, 2004, the Warrants shall be exercisable by the Warrant Holder into an aggregate number of shares (including those shares described in the preceding paragraph) of Company common stock equal to twenty-five percent of the number of shares of common stock into which the Series B Preferred Stock, held by such Warrant Holder, is convertible, calculated as of the closing of this Series B financing. In no event shall the Warrants be exercisable, in the aggregate, into a number of shares of common stock of the Company greater than twenty five percent of the number of shares of common stock into which the Series B Preferred Stock are convertible, calculated as of the closing of this Series B financing.

Voting and protective provisions Series B Preferred Stock votes on an as converted to Common basis, but also has a class vote, by 51% majority on altering, changing or amending the preferences, privileges or rights of Series B Preferred Stock.

TERMS OF INVESTOR RIGHTS AGREEMENT

Right of first offer on subsequent issuances The holders of Series B Preferred Stock who hold at least 200,000 shares shall have the right in the event the Company proposes to offer equity securities to any person (other than the securities issued pursuant to employee benefit plans or acquisitions, in each case as approved by the Board of Directors, including the director elected by holders of the Series B Preferred Stock) to purchase on a pro rata basis all or any portion of such shares.

This right shall not apply to the issuance by the Company of up to a number of shares, equal to 19.2% of the fully diluted shares after the offering of its Common Stock to employees, officers or directors of, or advisors or consultants to, the Company pursuant to its stock purchase or option plans. It shall also not apply to Common Stock issued in connection with strategic alliances or other partnering arrangements approved by the Board of Directors and other customary exceptions.

This right shall terminate immediately prior to (i) the closing of a Qualifying IPO; or (ii) the closing of any merger or consolidation of the Company.

Right of first refusal on sales to third parties by investors Pursuant to the Company's Bylaws, the Company shall have the right in the event a stockholder proposes to offer equity securities to any person to purchase all or any portion of such shares. Any securities not subscribed for by the Company shall be reallocated among the other stockholders on a pro rata basis. If neither the Company nor the other stockholders purchase all of such securities, that portion that is not purchased may be offered to other parties on terms no less favorable to the selling stockholder for a period of sixty days. Such right of first refusal will terminate upon a Qualifying IPO.

REGISTRATION RIGHTS

Company registration Unlimited "piggyback" registration rights subject to pro rata cutback at the underwriters' discretion. Full cutback on IPO, 25% minimum inclusion thereafter. If the Investors are so limited, however, no party shall sell shares in such registration other than the Company or the Investors, if any, invoking the demand registration.

S-3 rights Up to two demand registrations on Form S-3 per year; minimum offering size of $1,000,000.

The Company may defer an S-3 filing for up to 90 days once during any twelve-month period. No more than two S-3 registrations at investors' request permitted during any one twelve-month period.

Termination of registration rights Registration rights terminate (i) three years after initial public offering; or (ii) when all shares held by an investor can be sold under Rule 144 within a 90 day period.

No future registration rights may be granted without consent of a majority of Investors holding registration rights unless such rights are subordinate to those of the Investors.

Expenses The Company shall bear registration expenses (exclusive of underwriting discounts and commissions) of all such demand and piggyback registrations (including the expense of one special counsel of the selling shareholders). Investors bear the expenses pro rata of all S-3 registrations.

Transfer of rights The registration rights may be transferred to (i) any partner or retired partner of any holder which is a partnership, (ii) any family member or trust for the benefit of any individual holder or (iii) any transferee who acquires at least 100,000 shares of Registrable Securities, provided the Company is given written notice thereof.

Standoff provision No Investor shall sell shares within 180 days of the effective date of the Company's initial public offering and 90 days of any other public offering if all officers and directors are similarly bound.

Board representation and meetings The authorized number of directors shall initially be three. Effective upon the closing of the Series B Preferred Stock financing (the "Closing"), the members of the Board shall be Larry, Curly, and Moe.

Inspection and information rights All Investors holding at least 100,000 shares of Series B Preferred Stock shall receive annual audited and quarterly unaudited financial statements. Thirty days prior to the start of each fiscal quarter, the Company shall provide to such Investors a comprehensive operating budget forecasting the Company's revenues, expenses and cash position on a month-to-month basis for the upcoming fiscal quarter. Similar projections shall be provided for the entire fiscal year 30 days in advance of the start of the fiscal year.

TERMS OF PREFERRED STOCK PURCHASE AGREEMENT

Representations and warranties The investments shall be made pursuant to a Stock Purchase Agreement reasonably acceptable to the Company and the Investors, which shall contain, among other things, appropriate representations, warranties and covenants of the Company reflecting the provisions set forth herein and other standard provisions, and appropriate conditions to closing, including a customary legal opinion of Company counsel regarding the financing.

Expenses The Company and the Investors shall each bear their own legal and other expenses with respect to the transaction. Every effort will be made to minimize these expenses.

FOUNDERS AND EMPLOYEE AGREEMENTS

Stock vesting All stock and stock equivalents issued after the Closing to employees, directors and consultants shall be subject to vesting as follows: 25% to vest at the end of the first year following such issuance, with the remaining 75% to vest monthly over the next three years. The repurchase option shall provide that upon termination of the employment of the shareholder, with or without cause, the Company or its assignee (to the extent permissible under applicable securities law qualification) retains the option to repurchase at cost any unvested shares held by such shareholder.

Restrictions on Common Stock transfers No transfers allowed prior to vesting. Right of first refusal on vested shares until initial public offering.

Market standoff Holders of Common Stock and options must, at the request of the Company or an underwriter involved in the Company's initial public offering, agree not to sell or otherwise transfer any securities of the Company during a period of up to one hundred eighty days following the effective date of the registration of such initial public offering.

Proprietary information and inventions agreement Each officer, employee and consultant of the Company shall enter into a confidentiality, non-disclosure or proprietary information and inventions agreement as reasonably requested by management of the Company.

OTHER PROVISIONS

Expiration If not accepted by the Company by the close of business on March 1, 2002, this term sheet shall expire.

Closing conditions Closing subject to negotiation of definitive legal documents and completion of legal and financial due diligence by Investors.

Capitalization Upon the Closing of this financing the capitalization of the Company shall be as set forth on Annex A attached hereto.

Don't worry so much about what the first term sheet looks like, since the other VCs won't know the terms (unless you broke the first rule of never telling them to whom you are talking). Never say yes or no to the first term sheet. Thank the VC and tell her that you are expecting other term sheets shortly and you will evaluate her proposal.

You might also want to throw in that you were shocked by the low valuation, but you appreciate that this is a negotiation.

(Note: Never lie during the process. Don't give information if you don't want to give it, but never just make up information or it will come back to haunt you.)

Once you get a term sheet, tell all the other VCs that you have a term sheet. Hopefully, you'll get multiple term sheets, and then you can pick the best one. That is usually what happens, if you're lucky. Once a VC knows that someone else has put in an offer, he is more willing to make a commitment himself. Getting that first bid is the hard part. Once someone has stepped up to the plate and made an offer, all of a sudden you'll find there's more interest. It forces other people to take action, and the price invariably goes up.

You should hopefully have a number of term sheets after one or two months (unless it's August; like psychiatrists, all VCs take August off). It's probably best to decide on the highest-valuation term sheet from a reputable VC. Early in the negotiations, you want to negotiate with only a single VC. Tell the others that you would still like them in the deal, but their term sheet was not acceptable, and you're going with the best overall offer. If they want to match it, to get in on the offering, you'd be happy to have them.

All VCs will swear to you that their term sheet is the standard term sheet. "This is the way all deals are done," they'll say. "The form is just boilerplate." Try to keep a straight face when they say this. There is no standard term sheet.

Perhaps the most important term on the term sheet is "valuation." Never sign a term sheet that doesn't have an adjective in front of "valuation." Valuations are either premoney or postmoney. Let me give you a simple example of why those adjectives are so important.

Suppose a VC says your company is worth $10 million, and his firm is willing to invest $5 million. You might assume he means premoney valuation, which would result in the VC owning a third of your company. (The $5 million he puts in would raise the company valuation to $15 million, and his share would be worth 33.33 percent of the company.)

The VC will come back and say, "Oh no, we always talk in terms of postmoney valuation." Meaning he believes the $5 million he is contributing brings the value of your company up to $10 million. If that is the case, the VC owns 50 percent of your company ($10 million divided by $5 million). Make sure you know whether you're talking pre- or postvaluation on the term sheet.

If you have gotten this far, it's time to bring in one or more of the other VCs if you still need more financing. Sometimes, two to five VCs will form a syndicate to invest in your company. They will all invest on the same terms and conditions.

This is a key reason it's important to have a reputable VC as the lead investor. If a prominent VC agrees to invest, lots of others will follow. When we raised $40 million to help fund the growth of DoubleClick, Bain Capital and Greylock were our lead investors. Bain Capital is not strictly a VC, but it is a hugely respected investor and is moving into financing early-stage companies. Greylock is considered one of the top-tier VC firms. Four other companies invested fairly large sums of money with almost no discussion. One company invested $10 million based on only a thirty-minute conversation. The position of those five firms was that if Bain Capital and Greylock had investigated us and were willing to invest, they would be, too.

> Generally, I think it's better to have more VCs investing than fewer. The VC network is wide and deep, and the bigger your network is, the better luck you'll have in finding customers and employees down the road.

Just because you get everyone to agree to the term sheet doesn't mean you're done. It will take at least thirty days to complete all the contracts and agreements. Get yourself a good lawyer, one who has done VC deals. You'll need one.

Public Financing

It is hard to believe now because it seems so long ago, but the late 1990s were an unprecedented time for start-ups trying to raise money. I remember our decision to take DoubleClick public in mid-1997. It looked liked we would end the year with around $30 million in revenues, which is great for a start-up but not very impressive for a public company. Most people thought it was way too early to go out. They said we should wait at least a year before doing an IPO.

In hindsight, this conversation was pretty funny, since the revenue for future IPO companies continued to decline as the market grew progressively hotter. I remember one company having under $1 million in sales when they went public at the height of the dot-com craze.

Remember what we talked about earlier: The best time to raise money is when you don't need it. When we took DoubleClick public, we were in good shape financially. We didn't need the money. But people wanted to give us some through the IPO, so we took it. That allowed us to expand even more rapidly.

Spurred in large part by the run up of the stock prices of NASDAQ companies in the late 1990s, the public has taken a greater interest in funding early-stage start-ups. I suspect this horrible trend will quickly end after the public and the start-ups get burned a few more times. (The dot-com crash in 2000 may have been enough to do the trick. We'll see if watching the NASDAQ going from over 5,000 to under 2,000 in about a year is enough to cool off interest.) Going public too early is a bad idea. It's like getting married too early or having kids too early. It complicates things.

What happened during the height of the dot-com craze was moronic. The public became, in essence, venture capitalists—and they were bad VCs. There was no real financial scrutiny of the firms going public. Entrepreneurs were able to raise tens of billions of dollars for companies that never should have been funded. It was like randomly taking bands out of clubs and signing them to record deals. Once in a great while, you'll get lucky and find a U2, but that is not the way to bet—or to invest your money.

A company shouldn't go public if its future is reasonably unpredictable. I believe in the old system—with initial financing from family and friends, then angels and VCs, then going public only when there is a solid track record in place.

The decision to go public is a big one, but also a simple one. There are two chief criteria for going public:

1. Can you accurately predict revenue and expenses?
2. Do you need publicly traded stock for acquisitions or additional funds for expansion?

If you're thinking about going public, and your earnings are still largely dependent on one or two major companies, don't do it. The day you miss your numbers is the day your stock crashes and you lose all credibility with Wall Street. It will take years for your replacement to dig his way out.

There's no reason to talk any more about going public. You're a long way away from that day. When it comes, find yourself an experienced lawyer and investment banker and accounting firm. They'll help you figure out the process.

ABOUT PROFIT

I would imagine that 99 percent of corporate statements, goals, or principles have a line about how they are in business to make a profit. It's sort of like saying the goal of a basketball game is to win—of course it is.

I've always seen profit a bit differently. I think it's more important to consider how you can win.

Some people might be proud of building a profitable business quickly. But that shouldn't be your ultimate goal. Building a market-dominating company should result in your having created a large and profitable business. Companies that lead their market make huge profits—how can they not? The primary drive of most start-ups should be to dominate their market, by solving their customers' problems, rather than to get to profitability quickly.

Unfortunately, being aggressive and trying to lead a market is considered evil these days. I recently had a reporter do a hatchet job on me by accusing me of being an aggressive competitor. My sin, in his eyes, was that I push the rules limit. He tried to show that because I did this in wrestling and basketball, I also do it in business. A "passive" competitor isn't much of a competitor, is he?

As long as you play within the rules, you're okay in my book. One of your goals should be to lead your market. Don't worry about being broken up by the Justice Department because you have too much market dominance. Before you get broken up, you have to pass through the stages of "insanely profitable" and "super rich." You'll get over it.

Think about how much money you need to raise to establish a clear leadership position within your market. If you accomplish this goal, you'll be profitable.

THE PROBLEMS WITH MONEY

Up until now we have talked about the good things that happen if you are able to raise a lot of money. Let's end the discussion with a few words of caution.

Frequently, large cash infusions into a company can hurt it. Too often a start-up raises a lot of money, and the management confuses this with success: "Ah, we made it, now we have to start living like we made it." They go out and get grade-A office space and start flying business class. What a bunch of morons.

From day one, you should instill a sense of fiscal responsibility within the company, and that responsibility starts at the top. If you take a large salary and fly business class, then everyone else will expect to do the same. If you go with a caste system (only executives fly business class), you'll create a culture of corruption in which cheating and stealing become the norm.

My maxim about money is simple: Spend money *only* to make money. Every time you are about to spend money, ask if there will be a return on that investment. If the answer is no, don't spend the money. Every expense should be treated as an investment.

Take office space as an example. In the early stages, you can work out of a shack and it shouldn't matter. (We started DoubleClick in a basement.) Investors love to see you toiling away in working conditions that would make a fire marshal cringe. You don't have to worry about appearances, because you don't have any customers, and the people who are investing in you want to know that virtually all their money is going into creating the product. Investors hate to see waste. They want their money well spent.

As you obtain customers and they begin to visit the office, you'll want to upgrade your space. Customers want to do business with a stable company, so your office should give the air of stability. But nobody likes to do business with a company whose office space is too lavish. It gives customers the impression that you might be charging too much for your products.

Think of waste as a disease that will spread through your company. When the office space is lavish, employees will think it's okay to check in to lavish hotels and throw lavish parties. If a prospective new employee doesn't want to join because the office space isn't nice enough, then consider yourself lucky to have avoided contact with Typhoid

Mary. Remember, the point of raising money is not to spend it. It is to build the business.

I was always in awe of one Internet company that spent over $100 million in a single year. Do you know how hard it is to spend $100 million? That was quite an accomplishment. They're history now.

On a related note, you probably noticed that I made no mention of an exit strategy, a way to take the most dollars out of your business by either selling out or going public. That omission was deliberate.

First of all, I hate the term "exit strategy." It sounds like you're building a pyramid scheme or conducting a scam to beat your investors out of their money. I know that's not what the term means, but that's the way the whole concept feels to me.

It's probably important for you to talk about how your investors will eventually have the option to sell their investment if they choose. But I'll guarantee you that the founders of hugely successful companies— the ones that have stood the test of time—never talked about exit strategies. With top-tier companies, there are no exits. You hold on forever. After all, you have found a consumer need and figured out how to fill it efficiently.

And now you're funded!

SUMMARY

1. **Who better than you?** You can find your initial source of funding when you look in the mirror. It's you. Then you move on to family and friends, angel investors, and hopefully venture capitalists and other strategic investors.

2. **Don't hoard.** There is a natural tendency to hold on to as much of your equity as possible. Don't. Concentrate on building a successful venture. If you do, whatever percentage of the company you own will be worth a lot.

3. **Raise more than you need before you need it.** You can never have too much money when you are starting a company. And you want to have that financing in place before you are desperate to get it.

4. **Play fair.** Bend over backward to give your investors a good deal. It will generate goodwill, something you'll need when the inevitable rough times come.

CHAPTER

THE RIGHT PEOPLE:
HIRE SMART ATHLETES

Still looking for that SPECIAL someone?
—PERSONALS, *The Village Voice*

You have one last area to focus on: finding the right people to build and grow the company.

I don't care how smart you are, or what you've accomplished in your life, or how revolutionary your product concept is, great companies are built by teams of people and not solely by their CEOs or founders. (As we talked about in the last chapter, founders are seriously overrated.) In this chapter, I want to talk about how to hire, organize, and retain great people, because if you don't do all three of those things, ultimately, nothing good is going to happen. That is true for more established companies as well as start-ups.

With that by way of context, let's start here: You need to hire people smarter than you.

This is a pretty tough concept for most founders/entrepreneurs/ division heads/CEOs to understand. After all, they ask, how can anybody be smarter than they are? Weren't they the people who either came up with the idea for the business in the first place or have been running this part of the company successfully for a while? Who can be smarter than they?

Sorry, but we (especially entrepreneurs) all have shortcomings in many areas. It's important to:

- Understand what your shortcomings are
- Find people who complement or offset your weaknesses

I was good at crafting a very focused strategy and communicating it to employees, investors, the press, and customers. However, I'm not good at handling the execution.

People generally liked me (at least I think they did) and found me personable and unassuming when I was running a company. However, I don't like executing the tough decisions. For example, I wouldn't be able to make the staff reductions required to keep a company healthy in today's current economic environment. This is why it's important to find people who complement, not replicate, you. Kevin Ryan was a great replacement for me as CEO at DoubleClick.

Maybe you aren't good at operations and would have trouble managing a lemonade stand. Be honest with yourself. There is at least one thing, and probably a lot more than one, that you aren't an expert at or don't like to do. Compensate through the people you hire.

Most of us have trouble with this. It doesn't matter whether we're talking about people creating companies or people running established firms. They either hire people dumber than they are, so they won't feel threatened; or—and this is more common—they hire people they are most comfortable with who are almost identical to them in thinking and skills; or they hire people who will do their bidding.

These are all huge mistakes. If you are a founder, you need to hire people who have skills and abilities that can offset your weaknesses. That doesn't change once you become a senior manager of that firm or another established one. What this means is you need to spend a lot of time figuring out what you are and are not good at. Everyone has flaws. You need to figure out what yours are.

If you don't take this approach to building a company or something new within an established firm, one of two things will happen. Your initial investors will force you out of the top slot, and that's if you're lucky. Because if they don't fire you, the odds are your company will probably fail.

I was lucky. I figured this out in time. To the surprise of many people, I stepped down as CEO of DoubleClick in the summer of 2000, just five years after I cofounded the company. It wasn't an easy decision. I wrestled with it for a long time. I guess anyone would. As a cofounder, I viewed DoubleClick as my baby, and I had decided to turn my baby over to Kevin Ryan, our company president. But it was the right decision.

As I said at the outset, it is important for managers to know what they are best at. And the reality is that the odds are stacked against a founder running his company long-term. To be honest, I don't think that is a bad thing. For a company to not only survive but thrive, it needs to be run by the best possible person at each stage of its corporate life, and that may not be the founder (and definitely not her kids). I know that was the situation in my case. There were better people to run the companies I helped create, and I worked hard to make sure these people were given the top job. I'm an enlightened founder. I love to start companies. Running them long-term is someone else's strength. The most qualified person should hold the job. It is ability that matters, not longevity. That is something that founders need to understand.

If there is one point I have stressed throughout this book, it is this: You must focus on what is absolutely essential and ignore everything else. If you are going to innovate successfully, there is nothing more essential than building a great management team.

That is a concept truly excellent managers know, but it comes hard to entrepreneurs and innovators. An old saying goes, A managers hire A people, and B managers hire C people. Your goal is to get an A—or higher.

Ronald Reagan did. I always thought Ronald Reagan was a great president. My opinion isn't based solely on his politics but on the team he assembled. Reagan won't go down in history as the smartest president, but the man had an incredible ability to not only effectively communicate but also surround himself with good people who could implement his vision. That's great leadership. That's what you should be trying to do.

In 1983, the three of us who founded ICC were all in our early twenties. After the first year, we had about thirty employees, and we were starting to become—in our eyes, anyway—a "big" company. One of the best and most mature actions we took back then was to hire an experienced, and older, manager as company president.

Ideally, as we will talk about later, you want to be able to promote predominantly from within. But in your early days—especially if everyone in the company is relatively inexperienced—that may not be possible. That was the situation we were in when it came time for us to figure out who was going to lead ICC. We didn't have anyone who could do the job well. Instead of trying to continue to run the company on our own, we went looking for an experienced manager from the outside.

I remember when we first brought in Larry Duckworth to run ICC. I kept thinking about how old he was. (He was only thirty-five at the time. I just turned forty, so I must seem ancient to today's founders.) But Larry was an immense help in taking us to the next stage of becoming a professional organization. Under his direction, we continued to hire professional managers, and the founders worked in positions where they were best suited (as I mentioned earlier).

I took what I learned about hiring and creating organizations at ICC and built on it when starting DoubleClick. Even when we were just starting out, we already knew that we would build DoubleClick into a large company. Our primary focus was to create, right from the beginning, the human infrastructure that would be necessary to support rapid growth and a large organization. When we were hiring our first managers, we didn't go looking for people who could help run a hundred-person company. We wanted to find people who could run a thousand-person division on their own.

We were very lucky to find the management talent to support our growth, but it was a hard sell at first. We had just moved the company from Alpharetta, Georgia, to New York City (sounds like the movie *Midnight Cowboy*). I was less than a nobody. I had helped create a moderately successful business, ICC (albeit in an industry that no one knew about), but I didn't have any kind of track record in building a company that was going to be as big as the one we envisioned. What we had was the ability to offer people a senior place in a company that would be a major player in a new media, and a new media comes along only every fifty years or so. That proved very appealing, so we were able to attract the management talent we needed.

Without management talent, you will never grow, and you will never be truly successful.

How do you find the people you need? I don't think there is only one thing you can look or test for. But over time, I have developed my own checklist—actually two—that seem to work pretty well. The first deals with intelligence, the second with competitiveness. Let's deal with smart first.

START WITH SMART

I always look for people who are way smarter than average. If you go this route, of course, it means you have to figure what it means to be "smarter."

A lot of people confuse skills with intelligence. They think that because someone is a decent UNIX programmer, she would be a better hire for a programming job using UNIX than, say, an excellent Windows programmer. UNIX programming is a skill, excellence is a trait. Skills are easy to learn, and traits are impossible to obtain. Ideally, you want to hire a person who is very smart and possesses the skills you need. If you are forced to choose between skills and smarts, IQ always wins.

There are two reasons for that.

A smart person can learn anything. You can put him in a new situation—for instance, make someone who has never managed anything before head of a hundred-person department—and he will figure it out. He will not only determine what the department should be doing, he will also come up with an efficient way to run it. A less intelligent, though skillful, person will never become smarter.

Also, selecting smarts over skills gives you more options. If you hire specifically for skills, you limit the pool of people you can draw on.

Let me give you a quick example. A lot of new companies think they'll be going public at some point, and they say they'll only hire a chief financial officer who has previously done an IPO. That's ridiculous. Since not all that many companies go public, you're limiting yourself to maybe 1 percent of the CFO population. It's far better to hire the smartest CFO you can find. He will figure out the going public process. (I have gone through it twice. It's not that hard.) Smart people can handle whatever problems you face.

Why is intelligence the first thing I look for? Because it is the most necessary trait when you're creating something that hasn't been done before. New companies constantly encounter unknown events in their early years, and nobody possesses the skills to guide you through. You are pioneering new areas, otherwise you wouldn't have found customers for your idea. At DoubleClick, there were no business models in a media that was just emerging. We needed the smartest people we could find. Judging from all the failed Internet models, I'm glad we went down that path.

> **You need people who can figure out solutions to all the problems you are going to face. You need smart people.**

Okay, that's why smart is important. Now let's see if I can define smart. I think intelligent people can think logically and creatively, and they can apply this type of thinking to business situations; in other words, to real life.

Trying to figure out the smarts of the person you're interviewing is incredibly hard. Here are a few techniques I've come to depend on. There is no single screen, and none of the techniques is foolproof, but they are indicators of somebody's intelligence. However, the converse is true: If a person fails all the tests below, or even a majority of them, beware!

1. **Did he attend a good school?** Now, I know some of you are cringing (especially if you went to a bad school or you're a dropout; and remember, I'm not saying that one of these traits alone proves intelligence). But at the risk of being a snob, I will say there's a huge difference between going to the local community college and graduating from a highly competitive university.

The harsh reality is that our university system does a reasonable job of screening people. In general, highly intelligent people from any socioeconomic background can graduate from a competitive university. There are enough scholarships, grants, loans, and financial aid packages available to ensure that people with high IQs will have the opportunity to attend a good school. I have yet to meet a stupid person with a Harvard or Stanford MBA (as you'll recall, I have neither).

2. **How did she do at school; what did she do?** Their performance at the university might not be a very good indicator of intelligence. In fact, it might even be inversely correlated. Think back on the people you know who always got the best grades. Were they really smart, or obsessed with getting the best grades? Did they get the highest marks because everything came ridiculously easy to them, or did they just grind away at their studies? I like to see people who did more than produce good grades when they went to a good school. Did they have a job? Were they involved in any sports or groups? (That, of course, gets us to looking for competitiveness, something we will discuss next.) Bookworms tend not to be street-smart, even if they are grade-smart. That's why you want to look at what else they did at school.

3. **Have him explain your business.** Even though they'll know only a small amount about your company when they come in for an interview, smart people will have the uncanny ability to pick out the essential elements of what you do. They might get a few things wrong, but if they are smart, they'll at least be thinking in the right direction. They will have a solid handle on what your firm does, who it competes with, and what the business landscape looks like.

Less intelligent people will attempt to bullshit their way through the interview, or to seize on one unimportant aspect of your company that they might know something about, and become quickly befuddled when you ask them about anything else. It will be pretty embarrassing. Bright people will have figured out what is important.

4. **Pose simple logic questions to her.** Perhaps the easiest way to figure out a prospect's intelligence is to ask her some questions that test her reasoning. Management consulting firms such as Bain and McKinsey, and companies like Microsoft, use this technique.

What they—and I—do is ask people strange questions that are seemingly impossible to answer. For example:

- How many people die in New York City each day?
- How many gas stations are there in the United States?
- If you drop a cannonball off a rowboat over the deepest part of the ocean, how long will it take the cannonball to hit the bottom?
- Why are manhole covers round?
- How many gallons of water pass through the mouth of the Mississippi River every minute?

You aren't looking for the "right" answer. For most of these questions, there is no right answer. What you are looking for is:

1. Evidence that the candidate can identify the important variables needed to solve the question
2. Whether she can come up with a reasonable estimate in a reasonable amount of time

(In the "How many people die in New York City each day?" example, the biggest variable is not, as many people assume, the murder rate. Murder causes relatively few deaths. The biggest variables are overall life expectancy and population. If you know roughly how many people live in the city, say eight million, and you have a handle on how long people live on average, say seventy-five years, you can make a reasonable guess at how many people die each day.)

Again, you aren't looking for an exact answer, like "Two hundred ninety-two people die every day in New York." You are looking for the way people approach the problem.

Why go through this exercise? Why not let people go off and research the problem instead of putting them on the spot? There are a couple of reasons. First of all, everyone can get a perfect score of 1,600 on their SATs if we let them bring the test home and take as much time as they want to answer the questions.

But there is a more important reason. For most business problems, there are no right answers with 100 percent certainty. When it comes to the major decisions, you never have all the data you need. You have to be comfortable with that, because that is just the way it is. You have to take incomplete information and come up with the best answer you can, and that requires sound thinking and common sense.

That's what you're looking for here, though you don't always find it. When you ask people these kinds of logic questions, you'll get some pretty wild answers that will scare you.

When I was working in Georgia, I asked someone how many people died in Atlanta each day. His first response? He wasn't sure, but he knew how to find out. He'd follow all the ambulances in the city for a day. But then he said that wouldn't work because some of the bodies might be from Alabama.

When you get answers like that, don't hire those people. They probably don't have the level of intelligence you need. They're not meant to be your employees. They're meant to be your anecdotes.

FINDING ATHLETES

Smart is good. But smart in and of itself isn't enough. Unless people put that intelligence to use, no one benefits.

That is why, when I interview people, I also try to discover how competitive they are.

I look for four specific things.

1. **I love athletes.** Now, an athlete can be someone who has these traits but never competed in sports. What is important are the characteristics, not the varsity letter.

There's a pretty thin line between winning and losing in any sport. I remember vividly my first wrestling match. I was getting crushed. The other guy was faster and stronger and completely dominated me during the first five minutes. (And wrestling matches are only six minutes long.) Then a miracle happened. The other guy simply stopped fighting! In the last minute of the match, I pinned him and won.

I learned an invaluable lesson that day: Winners fight to the end.

In sports, we call the limit of somebody's ability to endure everything he is subjected to his "pain threshold." The theory says that the greater the person's pain threshold, the longer he will go on fighting.

In trying to create anything new, either a start-up or within an established business, you need to look for people with a high pain threshold.

An "athlete" could have been on the chess or debating team. The important thing is a continuous demonstration that they competed and won. If somebody has this trait, it will manifest itself somehow. If not, they don't have it!

The battle for a new market can be brutal. You need a cohesive team with a high pain threshold to wear your competition out, to make them quit. That's why you want athletes. When a smart athlete encounters a brick wall, she will find a way around it, or under it, or through it. She will bash her brains against that wall until the obstacle is overcome. Dwight Merriman, the cofounder of DoubleClick, is the best "athlete" I know. I have never seen a technical problem that he couldn't solve. When others would quit, saying the problem couldn't be solved or it would take too long, Dwight would always find a simple solution. Dwight would come in and not only get it done but do it in a week. If Dwight ran into a wall, he would go under it, around it, over it, and if those didn't work, he'd go through it. Great athletes love a big challenge.

Hiring smart athletes will dramatically increase your company's chances of success.

There is one other reason I love athletes. It is the trait that makes them so determined: a fear of losing. That's what drives most athletes—not the idea of winning but the fear of losing.

The same can be said about a lot of people who start or grow companies. They are afraid of failing, so they do everything in their power to make sure that doesn't happen. Like winning athletes, they will keep going until they find a solution or time runs out.

Ask yourself which feeling is stronger and longer-lasting, the thrill of victory or the agony of defeat.

Creating a new company requires people with a strong sense of commitment. Start-ups are a tough place, and you'll experience many turbulent spots and obstacles you could not have imagined, even if you spent ten years on your business plan. You can't afford to have people bailing out every time the company hits a bump in the road. That's a key reason you're looking for athletes. They've dealt with adversity; they've overcome tough times.

2. **Other signs of competitiveness.** Not all of us are athletes, so look for other clues as to whether the person is competitive. Perhaps he was on the debate team, or active in student politics, or captain of the chess team. The actual activity doesn't matter. The critical factor is: Was the activity competitive?

3. **What kind of companies did he work for?** Just like universities, good companies do reasonably well at screening for smart people. A résumé showing someone works for Goldman Sachs is better than an application from a person who works for the local bank. Working for Microsoft is better than having worked for a defunct software company. Also, look to see how fast she moved up in the organization.

You have to battle to get into a top company—they have more qualified applicants than they can hire—and you have to compete against other talented people once you are there in order to succeed. That's why asking where someone worked and how he did is a good indicator of how competitive he is.

> Past performance is perhaps the most important factor to examine in recruiting the best people.

4. **Avoid job hoppers.** I hate job hoppers, people who have had almost as many jobs—and, in some cases, more—than years of experience. I can understand a kid out of college making the wrong job choice once, even twice, but when you see somebody who consistently stays at a job one or two years before moving on, don't hire her. Send her on her way. There is no acceptable explanation for job hopping. In every case, it is an indictment of character.

It is possible that she'll say the reason she left her last job was that she didn't get the promotion she deserved. But the reality is that great people get promoted consistently, and bad people get passed over consistently. Virtually every person I've seen fired blamed everybody but themselves for being let go. We've managed to create a society where individual responsibility is an exception and not the rule. Look for the exceptions.

This one is easy. Don't hire job hoppers. Once your company hits bad times—and bad times are inevitable—the job hopper will be gone. And even if things go well at your company, the job hopper will be gone in a year or two, so why would you want to bother with him in the first place?

ODDS AND ENDS

There are a few other things I look for that go beyond being smart and athletic.

I am looking for someone with a passion for the business.

Once I was interviewing a Harvard MBA for a job, and I asked him what he thought about the possibility of working for DoubleClick. He told me it would be fine, "but it really wouldn't matter if we were selling nails. What is important is being in the game." Well, I appreciated his honesty, but he was the wrong person for us.

You need to feel passionate about what you do. One of my favorite studies of all time shows that whether employees are happy with their jobs has little to do with the job or the company they work for. How you feel about what you do for a living does involve your coworkers and your boss and the money you receive. But what the study showed—and what I believe—is that the biggest factor in job satisfaction is you. You have to believe in what the company is doing. Otherwise, you won't be happy.

A number of companies put a lot of emphasis on finding team players. You've heard the cliché: There is no "I" in "team." Well, I think the whole idea of teamwork is overrated. Yes, you want to hire people who can get along with others, and managers need to be team players. But the reality is that an individual created just about every major breakthrough.

If you are hiring someone, you want that person to believe that her job is going make a significant difference. If she doesn't, she probably isn't going to be happy.

My next point is something that a lot of people—especially people starting companies—find counterintuitive. There can be a huge advantage in hiring people away from big companies.

Start-ups are often leery of hiring people out of big corporations for fear that they are simply high-paid bureaucrats who won't get the start-up mentality. Well, there's a reason why big companies are big—they have smart people running them.

Without question, big companies employ some fairly useless people, but you can find some of your best and most mature talent from these companies if you do your research.

If you are worried about a prospect's ability to make the transition from large company to small, here is a method that I have found that works. Simply force her to trade certainty (cash) for a greater upside (options). You'll weed out bureaucrats quickly—they won't want to risk anything—and find true entrepreneurs, people who look for opportunity. Your goal is probably to become a big company yourself someday, so having people around who know something about running a big company is enormously valuable.

Two last points on this topic:

1. Don't hire a person if you don't think he can do the job.
2. Always ask, "Is this best possible person for the job?"

Both those things sound obvious when you put them down on paper, but sometimes people will say: "Anyone is better than no one" when they have a hiring need. That's wrong. The wrong person can cause a lot of damage, especially in the beginning stages of a company, when every move counts. You are better off waiting to find the right person.

Finally, I don't know how scientific this is, or even how you create a system for doing it, but here is my best hiring advice: Hire people you like. Assuming they have the traits you're looking for, if you like the person you hire, that helps a great deal.

When you're trying to get something off the ground, you'll be spending more time with these people than your wife or kids. You'll naturally work harder and better with people you like than those you dislike. Every time I've gone against this credo, I have regretted it. You will spend a lot of time with these people, and liking them will make your interactions a lot easier.

When you are growing a small business, it is all about the leverage. Find people who can get the job done and move on to the next challenge.

BUILDING THE ORGANIZATION

People in place, it is time to build your company or take on the new project within an established firm. I'd start with what former president George Bush called "the vision thing."

Founders often have great visions. Unfortunately, they often have more than one and don't communicate any of them well. You need to have a single vision, and you need to communicate that vision over and over and over again. One-on-one. In small groups and companywide. You have to keep repeating the message until everyone is clear on what it is.

You can reinforce that vision by involving people in the creation of the strategy that the company will follow to make your vision a reality. Using BPT to create the corporate strategy is extremely effective. People are far more interested in pursuing a strategy they helped to create than in being forced to support one they've had shoved down their throats.

One more thought before we get to creating the organization itself. Getting people to work hard is not the big issue; it's getting them to think big enough. We all look in awe at companies like Microsoft, Oracle, and Dell. They're so huge! There's no way, we think, we can ever build a company that big. If you don't believe you can build a large company, there's no way others will believe it, either. You first need to believe (really believe) that you can build a leading global company, and then you need to help others believe in the same vision.

Back in 1997, DoubleClick hired Chris Saridakis and David Rosenblatt to launch a new business called DART, which, to oversimplify, allows advertisers to deliver the most targeted advertising possible on the Web. As an example, you go to a search engine and type in "new cars," and an ad for Ford pops up. There were already a couple of companies doing this kind of thing, so we knew attaining the market-leading position would be an uphill battle.

Chris and Dave's first job was to create a business strategy. They came back a month or so later and presented a plan that called for them to hire between ten and twenty people. I told them I was impressed it would take that few people to lead the industry. Of course it would take more than that, they replied; those people were necessary to build a business, not to lead the industry.

I asked them to go back and create a plan that would make us the clear leader. Chris and Dave returned with an aggressive plan and went on to build a massive business, one that is now the definitive market leader.

Today Chris and Dave know only one way of thinking–HUGE! That is the way you have to think from the very beginning.

PUTTING THE STRUCTURE IN PLACE

We've talked about the kind of people you should hire; now let's talk about when. Hire people only when you need them. To oversimplify, you don't need a CFO before you have any revenue, and you don't need a public relations staff before you have anything that can be helped by PR.

Yes, you want to build an organization that is capable of dominating your industry, but you don't want to take on needless costs and create substantial overhead before you have to.

It's a trade-off, but in the beginning, you can buy the time of various experts–lawyers, accountants, and consultants of all types. You don't have to hire people full-time from day one.

Once you start building your organization and your firm starts to grow, you'll need some sort of formal structure. It can take one of three different forms. My belief is that all organizational structures are evil; the CEO needs to figure out the least evil organization for her company. You can organize by:

- **Function.** All the financial people work together and report to a finance manager; the human-resources people work together and report to the head of HR; etc.
- **Business unit.** People are organized into a mini company that has been created to sell a particular product or service to a specific market segment.
- **Matrix.** This is the structure for managers who can't decide if they want to organize by function or business unit. There are all kinds of dotted-line reporting relationships.

As I said, this is an issue only as you get bigger. No matter how you look at it, each of the three structures is flawed.

Every organization is evil. You must choose the least evil form.

It boils down to picking between efficiency and effectiveness. If you want effective, organizing by business unit wins hands down, especially if you're launching a new business. Business units are focused, and as I've repeated (probably ad nauseam), focus wins.

You can argue that organizing by function is more efficient. But it is rarely effective. One department usually can't accomplish anything by itself. Worse, being organized by department means your employees spend most of their time looking inward, instead of trying to figure out what the customer wants.

The matrix model should, in theory, be efficient and effective. But it has two primary problems. With everyone reporting directly to one leader—the head of their department—and indirectly to another—people in charge of various projects—things invariably get bogged down. Since decisions are constantly being sent up the chain of command, you have people who are further and further away from the customers deciding what needs to be done for them. Or you have two leaders coming out with different decisions, resulting in indecision.

People argue that business units are not particularly efficient, and they're right. After all, each unit could have its own person who handles finance, HR, receivables, administration, etc., instead of having those functions handled by a centralized department. Yet business units are the most effective at getting things done, because they're organized around selling a particular product or service.

Organize by business unit, especially when you are starting something new. Then figure out how to promote your best people as quickly as you can.

Find people you can trust. Then listen incredibly hard to them.

PROMOTE SMART ATHLETES

Ironically, nobody is qualified for a promotion. The whole point of a promotion is to move somebody into a new role that she's never occupied before, so, of course, she won't be qualified. The only way to become qualified is to be doing the job already, in which case there'd be no opening. This inherent irony is probably why everyone looks outside the organization when it comes time to fill senior positions. They go off searching for someone who has done the job before.

When you are first building, you need to create enough of a human infrastructure to contain the basic skills to run the company. If you are just starting out, you may be forced to go outside to find the talent you need.

However, if you have been in business awhile, my experience is that it's far better to promote a known person—with his shortcomings and all—than to hire a complete unknown who undoubtedly has shortcomings as well. As the old saying goes, "Better the devil you know."

The point? Promote your smart athletes as quickly as you can. Push these folks to the extreme, and they will rise to the occasion and surprise you. Rapid promotions send great signals to all your other smart athletes and give them higher goals to aspire to, and everyone, especially the organization, wins. We try to promote superstars as quickly as we can. We make sure they have the jobs they want. We hired Kevin Ryan as CFO, and he became president and then CEO in fairly short order while he was still in his thirties. David Rosenblatt moved from a staff position to running most of DoubleClick in just a few short years.

I know I've never been qualified for any of my jobs, but I've been smart enough to figure out what needed to be done. That should be true of all the people you hire as well.

That brings me to a point that should be obvious but far too often isn't. Seniority is irrelevant. You promote a person because she can do the job, or you are convinced she can do the job, not because she has been with you for a long time.

It is popular for people to wear an employee number below their name on their security badge. That number typically indicates when they were hired. The lower the number, the longer they have been with the firm. We don't do that, because when you were hired doesn't matter. What should matter is the kind of job you are doing for the company today.

"WE NEED TO TALK"

Invariably, a certain percentage of the people you hire will not work out. When that happens, you need to take action right away. Yes, you should sit down with the person, explain in detail what the problem is, and suggest specific courses of actions he can follow to get back on track. But you need to know going in that the changes probably won't occur, or probably won't occur sufficiently, to justify keeping him on the payroll.

When the second chance doesn't work, and my experience shows that it rarely will, you have to let him go. This is hard, and I am bad at it. You want to save people. No one likes to fire anyone. Still, there are times it has to be done.

If people are

- not hitting their goals
- constantly making excuses for not getting their work done the way it should be done
- consistently putting you and your company at a disadvantage

then you have to make a change—and the sooner, the better.

RETAINING YOUR EMPLOYEES

You've done an exhaustive search to make sure you've found exactly the right type of employees for your company. You've weeded out those who, for whatever reason, didn't fit. How do you go about keeping your best employees?

Clearly, compensation is important. But so is giving them ownership in the firm.

Let's deal with pay first.

What you pay people is not the most important thing about a job (or building an organization) but it is important.

There are two types of compensation:

- Certainty (cash)
- Upside (bonuses in the form of equity or options)

Depending on where you are in your development as a company should determine the amount of weight you put on each component. It's a balancing act.

In your early stages, offer the absolute minimum amount of cash compensation to your employees. We are talking about paying people a subsistence wage here, the absolute least they can afford to work for. You probably won't be able to afford to pay more than that, and the employees, if they are smart—and they should be, because that is the first trait you looked for—will want to share in the company's potential. They will want as much equity as possible. A subsistence wage should not bother them too much.

As the company matures and your mix of people expands to include more experienced employees, you'll need to move more weight toward cash, along with fewer options. (Older, more seasoned employees tend to come complete with families, and working for a subsistence wage will be less appealing to them, or not financially possible.)

Ideally, you want to pay as little cash compensation to people as you can get away with. I know this might sound a bit harsh, but if you look at the two (extreme) possibilities, you will understand why this is the case. If you don't pay enough, nobody (or worse, bad people) will take the job. At the other extreme, if you pay too much, your company never becomes profitable.

Compensation all depends on supply and demand. In times of full employment, you'll have to pay more; during recessions, less. Know that going in. Pay what you have to, but no more. Compensation rarely motivates people.

I believe *all* employees should have options, even if only a few. Options are not just a form of equity that generally gives employees a chance to buy company stock at (hopefully) a substantial discount to the market price; it is also what bonds employees to their company.

Let me make an analogy to explain why I think every employer should be a shareholder. Do you treat a rental car differently than your own car? Of course you do. You will protect your own car and treat it nicely, because you own it. You'll abuse the hell out of the rental (as long as they can't see the damage) because it isn't yours. (There goes my Hertz #1 Club Gold card.)

Making all employees owners changes their perspective about the place they work. You'd be surprised how much a receptionist who is an owner can positively influence the perception the outside world has about a company. Next time you encounter a nasty receptionist, ask if he is a shareholder. I guarantee he won't be.

Giving all employees options also means you can talk to them as equals. It sends the (correct) message that you are all in this together. In old-style companies, only the executives have options. Feudal systems are dead.

There is one last reason I like paying employees in stock. I want people to feel some pain. I want them to hurt–at least a little bit–if the company doesn't succeed. Their fate and their company's need to be intertwined.

I haven't seen a person yet who didn't want the maximum in cash *and* options, but you can't survive by doing both. In the early days, I would solve this problem by making the person choose between packages in which they received more cash at the expense of fewer options. When people are forced to value options through a trade-off, they will usually go for the options. If they go too much for cash, then rescind the offer! They aren't the kind of people who will help you achieve your goals.

Typically, nonfounding employees will receive from 10 to 20 percent of the company's outstanding shares in options. Years ago, I surveyed a number of VCs and companies to find out the going rate for option packages. I put together these guidelines for early-stage companies, i.e., prepublic companies:

Titles	Average Percentage of Outstanding Shares
CEO	4.00%
VP	1.50%
Director, senior management	0.36%
Senior engineer, manager	0.40%
Key people, top sales	0.18%
Sales rep, engineer	0.14%

THE BOSS'S ROLE IN ALL THIS

Finally, let's talk about the boss's role. Your job as the leader is to set the strategies and priorities of the organization and stay focused on the tasks at hand. You establish where the company is going, you're consistent about that, and you act with integrity.

Just about everything else is up to the people you hire.

SUMMARY

1. **Hire the smartest people you can find.** If you are forced to choose between someone with the perfect set of skills but only average IQ and someone who is very bright, go with intelligence. Smart people will figure out what needs to be done.

2. **Look for athletes.** Find people who are used to competing.

3. **Stay out of the way.** The boss's role is to make sure the organization is going in the right direction and to act with integrity, and to make sure the smart athletes she has hired have the resources they need to get the job done.

CHAPTER

EXECUTIVE SUMMARY:
PUTTING IT ALL TOGETHER

We've covered a lot in the preceding pages. Although I've talked about a lot of different ideas, there has been one constant throughout: Focus exclusively on what you need to do to be successful, and ignore everything else.

Let me practice what I preach in summing up. Here goes:

- **The odds are against you.** That is the first thing you have to recognize if you're going to try to create something from nothing.

  A couple of things follow naturally from that. First, you want to be passionate about whatever idea you come up with. It is bad enough to devote your life to an idea that probably won't work. It would be a tragedy if that idea weren't something you felt passionately about.

  Second, you need a way to try to tip the odds in your favor. That is what I did. I am basically a lazy guy. I am always looking for a better and more efficient way to do things, and that is why I came up with this process for creating something from nothing.

> I find that the best business books are obvious. But that isn't surprising. The fundamentals of what you have to do are so obvious that they almost always get overlooked.

- **Brainstorming Prioritization Technique.** If this book has one overarching message, it is this: Focus on what's important, and ignore everything else. BPT is designed to help you create many options, then quickly narrow down to a few essential areas where you need to concentrate.

  You don't have the time to sit around and wait for a big idea to bonk you on the head. Even if you did have that kind of time, and the idea actually hit you, one idea is probably not enough. You want to have as many ideas as possible so you can pick the absolutely best one.

  That's where BPT comes in. Get the right people in the room. Define the problem carefully, and spend up to twenty minutes brainstorming to get all the ideas out. Once you've exhausted the ideas, combine similar thoughts. Once the ideas are clear, divide the total number of thoughts by three. This is the number of votes each person can cast, and only one vote for an idea.

  Circle the top three to six vote getters. Ignore everything else. And begin your research.

  BPT allows you to get all the options on the table and lets you build consensus, since everyone had a say in the formulation of the ideas that got the most votes.

- **The idea.** Eventually, you choose one idea, and only one, to concentrate on. No one has enough energy, time, and resources (including money and good people) to develop more than one idea at a time. You need to focus, focus, focus.

  The best ideas solve a fundamental need—not a want but a need. People must truly need what you have. The bigger the need, the better your product or service must be at meeting it.

  The most successful ideas usually have a huge technology component. Technology always allows you to do something better, faster, and cheaper.

  Speaking of that, if your idea puts you up against an established competitor, you must be ten times better at one tenth the cost. No one ever switched away from a product or service he liked just because someone offered him an incrementally better deal. With the idea in place, now you need to create a strategy to bring your idea to market.

- **Strategy.** Here you focus on the fundamentals. What elements will your product contain? (Answer: only things people absolutely need. You save things that "would be nice to have" until version two or three.)

  To refine the strategy even further, apply BPT to each of the key decisions you must make about your product. Decisions such as:

  - How will you price it?
  - How will you sell it?
  - How will you position it?
  - How will you deal with competitors?

  The answers to all these questions make up your business plan. In that plan, you want an executive summary that is not only short—aim for a half-page—but tantalizing. The business plan will be pivotal in the next phase.

> **Business has always been about the basics.**

- Money

  Keep the following two things in mind:

  1. Always raise more—probably three times more—money than you think you will need. No company has ever had too much working capital.
  2. Always raise money when you don't need it. It is much easier to find then, and you will get much better rates. If you are desperate, never show it—people give quarters to desperate people.

  Where do you look for money? You start with yourself, then move on to family and friends. After that, you turn to angels and eventually (hopefully) venture capitalists. If you do really well, you go for an IPO.

- **People.** Hiring great employees to help you turn your dream into reality is the last piece of the puzzle. Look for the smartest athletes you can find. Smart, because smart people beat not-so-smart every single time; and athletic, because when the odds are against them, athletes won't give up. They will remain competitive. Often the company that can bear the pain just a little longer will win. That is why you want athletes.

A FINAL THOUGHT

As I've said, the odds are overwhelmingly stacked against you. Following these steps will push them a lot more in your favor, but the odds will still be against you. That's why you need to be passionate about what you do. It is better to be poor and happy than poor and miserable.

I'd wish you good luck, but luck usually has little to do with it.

APPENDIX

WRITING FOR MONEY:
How to Really Create a Business Plan

Throughout the book, we've talked about the importance of creating a short, focused business plan, a plan that spells out clearly what you hope to do. If you do it well, the plan causes potential investors to take out their checkbooks. It also motivates the best possible employees to sign on.

That is exactly what happened when we showed people the business plan for DoubleClick. (It took me only three companies to figure out what I needed to do.)

Let me show you what we did and explain why we did it.

CONFIDENTIAL[1] BUSINESS PLAN

DoubleClick, Inc.

"doubleclick.net delivers the most highly targeted advertising on the Internet"[2]

Contact Information
Kevin O'Connor[3]
e-mail: koconnor@doubleclick.net
Web: http://www.doubleclick.net

Overview[4]

The Internet is a worldwide phenomenon and offers some of the greatest opportunities in the computer industry. Today A. C. Nielsen estimates the Internet to have over 17MM Web users in North America alone. IDC

---

1 Before we let anyone read this, we had them sign a confidentiality agreement, but quite frankly, I think confidentiality agreements are a waste of time. It takes forever to get everyone to sign them, and it is almost impossible to track down a breach should it occur.
2 Most business plans don't have it, but they should. You want to tell people in a sentence located at the front of the plan what problem you are going to solve.
3 You want to make it easy for people to reach you. I have never understood why everyone doesn't put contact information on the first page. It seems like an obvious thing to do.
4 This is the first thing I look for when I am thinking of investing in a company. Just about every investor does the same thing. That's why this section has to be the sexiest thing in the document. Spend most of your time on it. Pull out the best things from each of following sections—product, position, pricing, etc. People have to understand the premise of the company, but you also want them to be excited about what you have.

   You can call it an "executive summary" or "the overview," as we did. It doesn't matter what you call it. Just make it short and sweet. Tell potential investors these three things: what problem you are really solving; how big a problem it is; and why you are the best company to solve it. People who are investing money are busy. They get hundreds of business plans every week. They are not predisposed to care about you. You must make them. Hook them with the overview to get them to read the rest of the document. It's foreplay.

projects the Internet to grow to over 100MM Web users during the next five years, while Hambrecht and Quist project 200MM Web users over the same time period. The Web has quickly become the number one application on the Internet. Web browsers allow users to access rich, graphical information on over 50,000 Web servers throughout the world.

Websites are struggling to find ways to fund their content development. The "everything is free" model of the Internet presents a real catch-22 for website developers: how to provide quality content for free and still remain in business. This dramatic expansion of Web users and the need for websites to produce revenue has spawned a new media for advertising. This year alone, there was an estimated ad space for some 500MM advertisements. In the year 2000, there will be over forty billion ad spaces for sale.

Internet advertising offers benefits that are revolutionary to the advertising world. Advertisers are able to more accurately determine *reach* based on ad impressions (times an ad is viewed) with a higher degree of confidence than traditional media. In addition, users are able to "click" on the ad to retrieve additional information and perhaps even order the product.

However, there are several major problems with the existing advertising model. There are thousands of small websites that simply are not capable of attracting advertisers. There are thousands of potential advertisers who are unable to easily locate and audit these small websites. Only the few highly visited sites have been successful at selling ads. The key problem and opportunity today is that advertisers have no mechanism other than crude site profiles to target their advertising. In short, the problems are too many advertisers, too many websites, too many users, no ability to target, and too much confusion.

Doubleclick.net[5] solves all the major problems in Internet advertising. Doubleclick.net facilitates the most targeted advertising available on the Internet. Imagine a TV program displaying a personalized ad targeted specifically at you, based on your profiles and interests. We have created the

---

5 You may have noticed we are called doubleclick.net throughout the business plan. Here's why. When we started, somebody else owned doubleclick.com, and since our first product was DoubleClick Network, we used doubleclick.net. Today people refer to us as DoubleClick. (We bought the ".com" extension in the mid-1990s.)

most extensive user and organization profile database on the Internet. Advertisers are able to create a profile that best matches their target prospect for a specific ad campaign. When a user accesses a website that is a member of doubleclick.net, we dynamically display the ad that best matches the user or organization profile. doubleclick.net allows advertising to quickly determine and control the optimum *frequency* of an ad required to induce a response and to track responses. This unprecedented system provides advertisers with the ability to conduct a very targeted and cost-effective Internet advertising campaign. doubleclick.net provides advertisers with all the benefits of direct marketing, but at the price of advertising.

Websites benefit tremendously from doubleclick.net as well. double click.net automatically and dynamically displays an ad matching an advertiser's target prospect profile when a user accesses a doubleclick.net member website. The websites immediately start generating revenue the moment they become members of doubleclick.net and ads are displayed. A significant percentage of revenue is distributed to doubleclick.net members to encourage membership. doubleclick.net allows websites to focus on content development to attract more users rather than trying to drum up ad sales to support the website. Even Web users benefit. We live in a world where indiscriminate advertising is everywhere. With doubleclick.net, users view ads that are relevant to their environment and interests.

We believe doubleclick.net is an excellent opportunity. We are solving a fundamental problem in one of today's fastest-growing industries. Through the merger of the number one sales and marketing organization, Double-Click (previously a division of Poppe Tyson[6]), with the number one technology provider, Internet Advertising Network, DoubleClick is clearly positioned to lead this new market.

We are confident we can capitalize on this market.

---

6 Poppe Tyson was a small agency owned by BJK&E, the large agency holding company. They had a four-person media sales group within a division called DoubleClick. We merged with the DoubleClick group in January 1996 to form DoubleClick, Inc.

Internet Advertising Market

The Trends

The Internet is a worldwide phenomenon and offers some of the greatest opportunities in the computer industry. The Web has quickly become the number one application on the Internet. According to a recent Nielsen survey, there are over 17MM Web users in North America. This core group includes corporations, universities, and other organizations who have direct TCP/IP access to the Internet. According to Goldman Sachs,[7] approximately 9MM users have access to the Internet through online service providers (OSPs). Growth rates for the Internet and OSPs range from 40 to 100 percent each year. We use 50 percent growth for our projections.

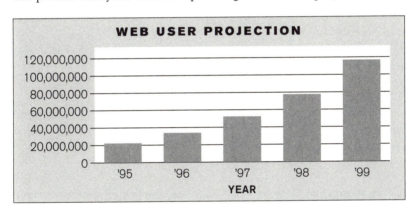

By the end of 1994, there were over 30,000 websites, with 1,500 new websites added to the Internet each week. We expect the growth rate of websites to be about 50 percent each year over the next five years.[8]

---

7 Busted, I know. Throughout the book, I downplayed the importance of experts. And I still think you can be led astray by their opinions. In fact, if you aren't *the* expert in your field, something is wrong. That said, I quote experts in the business plan because people tend to listen the them. Since that is the case, I often use "expert" opinions to support my own views. I definitely listen to experts, but I always take their views with a grain of salt. They are just another input. I don't let them unduly direct my opinions.

8 You'll notice the graphics get the point across, but they aren't overly slick. Too much of anything is bad. Don't be a slob, but don't put together a big production. Business plans are the art of the subtle.

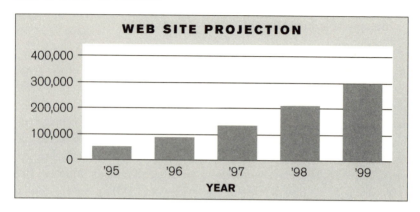

The general consensus is that the Internet is real and growth is explosive. If you use the Internet, you know and believe. If you do not currently use the Internet, you need to connect and see the vast potential of this new market.

The Problem

The perplexing question of the Internet, specifically the Web, is quite simply "How do you make money?" Without economic incentives, growth of the Internet, particularly in the area of content, is unsustainable. We believe there will be four economic classes of Web servers:

1. **Free information.** Organizations will use the Web to complement existing forms of communications, like telephone, mail, and BBS systems. The Internet offers an inexpensive means for delivering marketing information and customer services. Many companies already maintain a website, including Microsoft, Attachmate,[9] Coke, Ford, and IBM.[10]

2. **Transaction-supported.** For companies that take orders over the Internet, the service is simply a cost of doing business. Advertising is an opportunity for these companies as well. There are many online stores today, though early reports indicate few have been successful. The

9 As you may remember from an earlier discussion, our company, ICC, was bought by DCA. DCA merged with Attachmate in 1995.
10 As with any reference, it helps if people recognize the names.

Internet Shopping Network (now owned by the Home Shopping Network) is an example of a transaction-supported site.

3. **Subscription-based.** Just like the online service providers, these organizations make money from user subscriptions. To date, there are relatively few subscription-based servers. The need for the user to pay for and maintain separate accounts with each server is a major headache. *Individual*, *The Wall Street Journal*, and even *Penthouse* all have subscription-based websites.

4. **Advertising-supported.** These Web servers will offer the user valuable services or content (like a search server or publication) and generate revenue through advertising. One important feature of Internet advertisements is that the user can immediately acquire more information about the advertised product by simply clicking on the ad. Whether enough consumers follow the link or ignore the advertisement is not known, though we suspect in many cases, the user will take the link if the ad is relevant. Lycos and Yahoo! are examples of advertising-supported websites.

The Opportunity[11]

We believe advertising will become the major source of revenue for a large class of websites. To date, people typically obtain information for free on the Internet. Advertising supports this information-is-free model. The demographics of the Internet are quite impressive. According to a recent Georgia Tech survey, the average income of an Internet user was greater than $50,000, the mean age thirty-five, and the vast majority had college degrees. The Internet represents a very attractive audience for advertisers.

However, there are several major problems with the advertising model. There are thousands of small websites that are not capable of attracting advertisers. There are thousands of potential advertisers unable to easily locate and audit these small websites. Only the few highly visited sites have been successful in selling ads. Today advertisers have no mechanism other

---

11 You'll notice we used simple, straightforward language throughout the plan. No buzzwords. At best, jargon is often a crutch, and at worst, something to hide behind. I get business plans that string together buzzwords without telling the reader what the business does do! That's sad.

than crude site profiles to target their advertising. In short, the problems are too many advertisers, too many websites, too many users, no ability to target, and too much confusion.

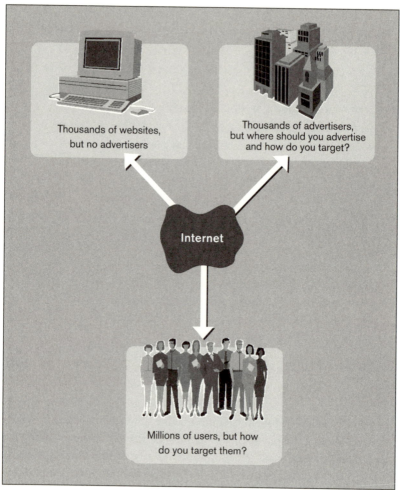

The general price model evolving for Internet advertising is price per *impression*. An impression is a onetime retrieval of an ad by a Web browser for display. Depending on the placement of the ad, the ad has a high probability of being seen. A website can track the number of impressions; and a number of auditing tools, such as I/PRO, are available to accurately count impressions. These same auditing tools also give very crude analyses of website profiles. The average price per impression is typically in the range of two to three cents.

Forrester Research estimates that companies will spend $10MM to advertise on the Web this year. Forrester predicts Internet advertising revenue to hit $2.2 billion by the year 2000. Below is our forecast for all Internet-based advertising over the next five years, considerably more conservative than Forrester's:

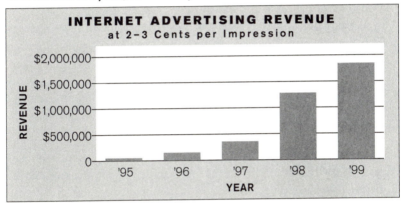

INTERNET ADVERTISING REVENUE
at 2–3 Cents per Impression

	Growth	'95	'96	'97	'98	'99
Total web users	50%	23,000,000	34,500,000	51,750,000	77,625,000	116,437,500
Average pages per day		3	5	7	9	11
Percent pages displaying advertising	4%	7%	9%	11%	13%	
Average cost per impression		0.02	0.03	0.03	0.03	0.03
Total market revenue		$20,148,000	$132,221,250	$356,997,375	$841,493,813	$1,823,236,594

The above projections are largely driven by four variables:

- Growth of Internet users
- Average number of Web pages read per day
- Ad cost per impression
- Percentage of Web pages displaying ads

There is strong consensus on the growth of Internet users. In the Georgia Tech survey, 72 percent of all respondents use their Web browser at least once a day, while 41 percent use their browsers six to ten hours each week.

The recent Nielsen survey found that the average Web user spends over five and a half hours each week using a Web browser.

It is difficult to compare an Internet ad to a more traditional print media or broadcast ad. However, our estimates show a print ad runs around ten cents for an impression. The cost of two cents per impression for Internet ads appears to be very inexpensive, and we feel this price will rise with the ability to target users. We forecast a conservative percentage of pages with ads, though we feel this number is potentially higher, given the attractiveness of advertising to sites as a way to gain revenue.

In short, websites need advertisers. Advertisers require the ability to easily and inexpensively target their advertising to a broad base of Internet users accessing a variety of websites. We are dealing with enormous numbers that are growing considerably each year. The infrastructure is in place to support advertising. However, no vehicle is in place to support the logistics of Internet advertising on a large scale. doubleclick.net is that vehicle.

The Solution

doubleclick.net brings advertisers, websites, and users together on the Internet. doubleclick.net facilitates the most targeted advertising available on the Internet. We are creating the most extensive user and organization profile database on the Internet. When a user accesses a website that is part of double click.net, we dynamically display the ad that best matches the user's profile.

Advertisers are able to create a profile that best matches their target prospect. The doubleclick.net server automatically displays the ad to a user matching the target profile when the user accesses a doubleclick.net website. This unprecedented system provides advertisers with a highly targeted and cost-effective Internet advertising campaign.

Websites benefit tremendously from doubleclick.net as well. double click.net automatically and dynamically displays an ad matching an advertiser's target prospect profile when a user accesses a doubleclick.net website. A website has the potential to immediately start generating revenue the moment it becomes a member of doubleclick.net by making simple HTML changes to its existing Web pages. A further benefit to doubleclick.net websites is that a large percentage of the revenue is distributed to doubleclick.net members. doubleclick.net allows websites to focus on content development to attract more users rather than focusing on sales of ads to support their server.

The users benefit also. We live in a world where indiscriminate advertising is everywhere. doubleclick.net exposes users to ads that are relevant to their interests. This targeted advertising will result in a higher percentage of ad jumps. The following is a high-level diagram of how doubleclick.net works:[12]

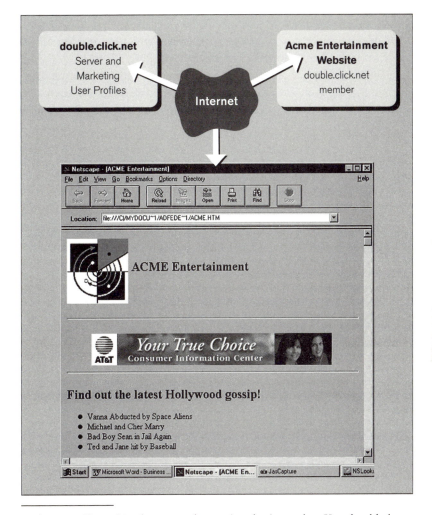

---

12 As you will see, it's okay to use humor in a business plan. You should always have fun.

We believe doubleclick.net is the missing component required for successful Internet advertising.[13] Through doubleclick.net, we can deliver an incredible number of ads with a very specific target profile through a diverse group of websites. Because of these factors, we believe doubleclick.net can secure the leadership position and be the standard in Internet advertising.

Below, we project a 9 percent[14] market share for doubleclick.net by 1999.[15] The first graph bar represents gross revenue to doubleclick.net. The second graph bar is the net revenue to doubleclick.net after revenue-sharing with the websites. Since our primary goal is to secure market share, we have a generous revenue-sharing arrangement with websites.

We have assumed that a full 50 percent of the revenue is disbursed to websites in relation to the number and price of ads placed on a particular website.[16]

---

13 There's a big difference between excitement and hype. Potential investors like to see excited entrepreneurs. At best, hype is essentially overstating the truth, and at worst, it's fraud. It's okay to be excited. It's not okay to hype.

14 Realistic expectations are vital. The most important thing a business plan does is measure the founder's IQ. One company gave projections showing it would be the fastest-growing and most profitable company in history. What was the probability of that happening?

15 You'll notice there aren't a lot of other financial projections in our plan. I have nothing against laying out a full page of numbers, if that is what will bring potential investors aboard. It can be done pretty easily. But I think the numbers we presented here are the most relevant ones; they gave a good idea of what the business would truly be about.

   The way we constructed our business plan is consistent with the whole premise of the book: There are a hundred things you could do and maybe five things you really need to do. Investors don't want to hear about the hundred, just the five.

16 You'll notice that we didn't go far into the future on the financial projections we did use. Projections depend on the maturity of the market. It's easier to forecast energy consumption or housing starts than a market that doesn't exist (like the Web back in the early-to-mid-1990s). Going over three to five years in a new market is pretty worthless.

   What's more important than the actual projections is the thinking behind

IAF BUDGET FORECAST[17]

Advertising Examples

Perhaps the best method for demonstrating doubleclick.net is through examples. We have selected a number of actual companies and designed fictitious advertising campaigns.

Attachmate

Attachmate, our previous employer, is the sixth largest PC software company in the world, with a wide variety of enterprise-communications

---

them. As a potential investor, you want to know, "Do the entrepreneurs fully understand the variables affecting their business?" The fundamental problem of most Internet companies was that they didn't have a basic economic understanding of their business. For example, if it costs you more to acquire a customer than the expected lifetime value of that customer, you have a bad business. Or, if you have negative gross margins (a new economic concept), you are an idiot (and the people who read that and invested are even bigger idiots).

17 IAF stands for Internet Advertising Federation, which was the first name for DoubleClick Network. The table shows our basic business model.

software products. Attachmate desires to go public over the next six to nine months; however, they lack significant name recognition. In addition, Attachmate has a major Internet-based strategy they want to publicize quickly. With doubleclick.net, Attachmate could perform the following:

- Target an ad ("Who is the fifth largest PC software company in the world?") for all brokerage employees, since they will ultimately be responsible for recommending Attachmate stock. In addition, we would target all publications and analysts with the same ad, since they will be writing about Attachmate.
- Target the Attachmate consumer Internet product at all AOL, Prodigy, and CompuServe users, since they are most likely to upgrade to a full Internet product.
- Target all users from the Global 5000 running Windows 95 with an ad for the new Extra Personal Client for Windows 95 product.
- Target all UNIX users with ads for the new X terminal product.

Microsoft

Microsoft is currently conducting a massive advertising blitz to upgrade Windows 3.1 users to Windows 95. Over time, Windows 95 advertising will need to become more focused. With doubleclick.net, Microsoft can target a Windows 95 upgrade ad to only Windows 3.1 users.

- For Windows 95 users, Microsoft could target Windows 95 upgrades for all their other applications, like MS Office.
- For Windows NT users at large companies, Microsoft could target BackOffice ads.
- For all UNIX users, Microsoft could target NT ads.
- Whenever Microsoft is conducting a seminar in a particular area, they could conduct saturation advertising for all Windows users in a specific geographic territory.

1-800-FLOWERS

1-800-FLOWERS wants to conduct a real-time advertising campaign that accomplishes the following:

* Saturation advertising in the week before Mother's Day
* Advertise only during business hours
* Regulate advertising to control call flow

Only with doubleclick.net can they can accomplish their ad-campaign goals. We can dynamically control the flow of advertising as well as control time and date for ads.

Delta Airlines

Delta is about to open a new nonstop route between Atlanta and Moscow. They would like to target their advertising to businesses in these geographic areas. doubleclick.net can target users who live or work in Atlanta or Moscow, and no matter what Web servers they access, the Delta ad is displayed.

Internet Security Systems

ISS is a small software company with a tool that allows companies to find network security holes before the hackers do. With doubleclick.net, they could focus their advertising dollars by targeting their most likely prospects: large companies running UNIX systems. An ISS ad would be displayed to users running a UNIX computer from a company with revenues over $100MM who access a website that is a member of doubleclick.net.

Interior Audio Design (IAD)

IAD is a small Atlanta-based company specializing in high-end audio and home theater equipment. With doubleclick.net, they are able to easily target all professionals working in a specified range of zip codes.

Positioning

We position doubleclick.net to two audiences: advertisers and websites. Advertisers are the key customers and will be the most difficult to obtain. Within an ad agency, the media planners and account executives are our primary prospects. We need to position this new media as similar to other types of media (like cable network or print). Our positioning statement for advertisers is:

"doubleclick.net delivers the most targeted advertising on the Internet"[18]

For advertisers, the key features and benefits doubleclick.net offers are:

Feature	Benefit
Ability to highly target users	• Dramatically reduces costs over nontargeted advertising • Ability to better control test ad campaigns • Regional companies are now able to cost-effectively advertise on the Internet • Higher percentage of users following ad jumps
doubleclick.net Internet Profiles Database	• Highly targeted and highly accurate placements of ads resulting in more effective advertising
Reach—impression tracking	• Advertisers pay only for ads displayed by users' Web browsers • High probability of ad being seen by user

---

18 Have we mentioned this before? You bet. Focus on a few things that are important, and repeat them throughout the business plan to drive home the message.

Feature	Benefit
Able to control frequency	• Advertiser is able to determine optimum ad frequency to induce a response and strictly control ad frequency to target market • Quickly determine effective exposure • Eliminates reach duplication
Central location	• No longer a need to deal with potentially hundreds of individual websites for ad placement and auditing • Focus your attention on targeting users, not websites
Real-time interaction	• Able to dynamically create highly targeted ad campaigns with immediate results • No more closing dates; initiate and modify ad campaigns interactively
Ad jumps—doubleclick.net tracks all jumps to your ad, along with detailed user profiles	• Provides you with critical information on what target ads are working • Quickly determine effective exposure • Refine target ads to reduce costs and make ad campaigns more effective • Advertiser can present virtually unlimited amounts of product information, even place orders directly
Detailed reporting	• Advertisers will have highly effective tools to measure the success of their ad campaign
Website selection and/or restriction	• Select websites with high affinity for target market • Able to target specific websites or restrict categories of websites or specific websites from displaying ad (competitor, content)

Key Advertising and Direct Marketing Measurements and Attributes

Key Measurement or Attribute	What Is It?	Problems with Traditional Media	doubleclick.net Strengths
Reach	• A measure of how many individuals were exposed to an ad	• Very difficult to measure, based on averages and probabilities • Significant amount of waste, more difficult to target	• Able to very accurately determine if an ad has been displayed, stronger probability ad was seen • Supports highly targeted ads
Frequency	• Number of times individual was exposed to ad; important for determining optimum exposure to induce a response	• Based on probability, lots of waste with overexposing and diminishing returns with part of the audience	• Able to easily determine optimum exposure and control ad frequency
Targeting or concentration	• Ability to narrow advertising to a target group based on profiles or affinity	• Direct marketing most effective for target advertising • Potential for a lot of waste, depending on target size and vehicles available • Could require management of large number of vehicles to reach target market	• Able to easily control profile information, access to large database of affinity (interests) information • Central location to target ads • Many of the characteristics of direct marketing but price of advertising

Key Measure-ment or Attribute	What Is It?	Problems with Traditional Media	Problems with Traditional Media
Test marketing	• Ability to test ad strategy based on target audience, ad offer or format, and creative styles	• Costs money and takes considerable amount of time	• Easy to test a number of variables to quickly establish optimum ad strategy
Personalization	• Ability to customize message for specific target groups	• Direct marketing is best suited for this • Expensive to create large number of ads	• Able to dynamically determine user profiles and present appropriate ad
Immediacy	• Key in direct marketing, asking for the order and fulfilling it	• Direct marketing is expensive (>.5 per individual) • Can't automate fulfillment	• Very inexpensive • Place orders directly online, less money, more immediate
Response tracking	• Key for direct marketing, track recency, frequency, source, and product line	• Must buy list from brokers	• Immediate access to users, associated profiles, recency, frequency, source, and product line interest

Websites

We feel we offer a no-lose opportunity for websites. Even if a website is already advertising, we provide it the means to sell unused ad space. There is virtually no effort involved with becoming a member of doubleclick.net. For websites, the key features and benefits doubleclick.net offers are:

Features	Benefits
Central location for advertisers	• Immediate access to large number of advertisers • Reduce sales and marketing expenses • Increase ads displayed, increase revenue and profits • Allows you to focus on better content, which will draw more users (more ads and more profit)
Revenue sharing	• Converts empty ad spaces into potentially valuable ad spaces • doubleclick.net targeting ability brings more revenue per ad, resulting in more revenue per ad for website as well
Nonexclusive	• Keep existing advertisers and supplement ads with doubleclick.net • Reduce empty ad spaces, increase revenue and profits
Reciprocated website advertising	• Free advertising for your website reduces marketing costs, increases traffic, increases ad space, and results in higher profits
Simple to join	• Everything is online, so you can join now and quickly begin receiving ad revenue
Simple modification to existing HTML documents	• In a matter of minutes, you can make the changes to your Web pages to begin receiving doubleclick.net ads and ad revenue
Set advertiser restrictions	• Able to control which advertisers or categories of advertisers are not allowed to advertise on your website (competitor or ad content issue)

Ironically, the largest problem with doubleclick.net is its broad market appeal.[19] There is a significant risk of spreading too thin and chasing too many unrelated markets without building a critical mass in any of them. Considering the existing demographics of the Internet, along with the functionality of doubleclick.net, we believe these categories will be our initial affinity groups:

- Technology
- Financial
- Entertainment
- Travel

The computer industry is the early adopter of the Internet and will be our primary target for the first year. In the Georgia Tech survey, 31 percent of the respondents were in a computer-related field. With so many websites on the Internet, there is an opportunity to actually advertise on other websites, like shopping networks and even company sites. Because of the ability of doubleclick.net to target consumers and their location, travel and entertainment advertisers will find doubleclick.net attractive. The tobacco industry is an interesting possibility, with their new restrictions on advertising: Since few laws appear to govern the Internet, this could be a prime advertising vehicle for them.

---

19 Our fear was that the market we were addressing was so big that a small start-up would have a difficult time securing the leadership position—guess we were wrong!

Product

doubleclick.net product performs two essential functions: managing the system and ad delivery. Most of the processes depicted in the architecture diagram below are for managing the system to effectively deliver ads to the appropriate target user. Only the ad server process delivers the actual ad to the user and handles ad jumps.

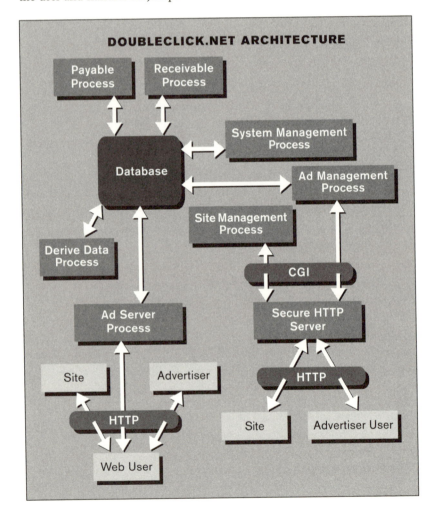

doubleclick.net Architecture

Following is a description of each of the processes shown above.[20]

Derive Profiles Process (DPP)

Building a comprehensive and accurate user and domain profiles database is fundamental to targeted advertising with doubleclick.net. We term this database the internet profiles database (IP-DB). We are able to compile a variety of information about users and entire domains. A domain is typically a network owned by an organization (for example, a company, university, or government) or division of an organization (for example, a company subsidiary, department, or agency). Like users, domains will develop certain profiles that are vital in targeting ads. In many cases, we can develop profiles about individual users. In other cases, we will fall back to the domain profiles.

We are able to tell an astonishing amount of information about a user. For example, we can determine operating system, location, organization type and name, company profiles, interests, and probability of following an ad jump, to name a few. We will not detail here how we are able to compile the IP-DB, since this is a trade secret. Suffice to say that we use a number of Internet and non-Internet sources of information to develop profiles about users and domains. The derive profiles process is the black box that develops the IP-DB. We can compile a very comprehensive initial IP-DB, then refine and add information as more and more users view doubleclick.net ads. The IP-DB becomes more accurate and complete as doubleclick.net becomes more successful. Thus, the IP-DB continues to create an ever larger barrier to entry for competitors.

Following is a more detailed list of the information we will track for each user and domain:

---

20 Why devote this much space to our technology? It's simple. Technology companies need to put up barriers to entry. Simple technology is simple to copy; complex technology is virtually impossible to copy. People want to invest in companies with potentially huge barriers to reduce competition (and thereby price erosion). The more you can convince them you have defensible technology, the better. That's why we devoted this much space to technology.

Variables

Domain name

Domain type:

    Online service (i.e., AOL)

    Dial-up ISP (i.e., Netcom)

    Commercial

    Education and level

    Government

    Military

Geographic location

Company information:

    Revenue

    Number of employees

    Primary SIC

    Secondary SIC

    Location

Operating systems

Browser type

IP address

IP address uniqueness

Access times

Frequency

Gender

Title

Areas of interest

Duration of page visits

Probability for taking specific types of ad links

Connection throughput average

Ads already seen

User and Domain Profile

Some of the data described above are "fuzzy." In many cases, we will know the data exactly; in others, we will have a high probability of knowing the data, or the data might be unknown. For example, most Web browsers tell us their type of operating system. However, for users coming in from America Online (AOL), we do not know what operating system they are running because the AOL browser does not relay this information. However, since the AOL user base is composed of typical consumers, they are probably running Windows.

Ad Management Process (AMP)

Advertisers must register their ad campaigns with doubleclick.net. They will interactively create target user profiles by selecting specific criteria. To target ads, the advertiser will be able to select criteria from the user and domain profile described above, as well as the website profile described below. The AMP will forecast the number of likely impressions (based on historical data) and cost per week. The advertiser can also control which websites are allowed to display the ad. Advertisers will be able to set an upper bound on impressions, so they will never exceed the cost estimates. If the ad campaign ends and doubleclick.net was not able to deliver the specified number of impressions, we will pro-rate the cost of the ad campaign.

The ad-estimate part of AMP is no trivial task. We will be dealing with millions of records of historical data, a large set of criteria, and some of the data is fuzzy. We will need to be able to make a highly probable estimation within five to ten seconds of a request. We will track information for each ad placed on doubleclick.net. Specifically, we will track:

Variables
Category of ad
Allowed sites
Ad jumps taken
Ads viewed by site
Ads viewed by user/domain
Price per ad

Ad Variables

Website Management Process (WSMP)

Websites must first register with doubleclick.net. We need to profile the website to better match ads and to enable the website to control the types of ads displayed. The website will specify which URLs will contain ads. Websites must make minor additions to display doubleclick.net ads. When the website activates those modified pages, they begin to benefit from doubleclick.net-placed ads. doubleclick.net will track statistics for each site, specifically:

Variables
Aggregate of user variables
Content category
Metrics versus other sites
Ads displayed
Page stats (per URL):
   Hits
   Date
   Time
   Duration
Number of visits
Duration of visit
Allowed advertisers
Regional/local interest

Website Variables

Ad Server Process (ASP)

The ASP is the heart of the doubleclick.net system. This is the real-time process matching millions of user requests with an appropriate advertisement. The ASP is essentially a stripped-down HTTP server that is highly tuned to quickly match ads and log transactions.

There is never unused ad space. If no *target* ad matches the user profile, we try to place a *remnant* ad. Remnant ads are lower-cost ads that are less specific about the intended target (hence the term). If there are no remnant ads, we will place either a doubleclick.net website ad or a doubleclick.net ad. This results in maximum revenue capability for doubleclick.net websites and provides them and doubleclick.net with free advertising for unused ad slots.

The ASP is also responsible for tracking and performing ad jumps. Ad jumps occur when a user selects a displayed ad for additional information. ASP tracks which user received which ad and from which website. Ad jumps are one of the most attractive parts of Web advertising, and keeping detailed statistics is essential.

System Management Process (SysMP)

doubleclick.net personnel run SysMP to perform systems management functions. These management functions include enabling ads, site approval, and database maintenance.

Payable and Receivable Processes (PRPs)

Both of these processes are noncritical to the functioning of double click.net. Initially, we will perform these functions manually until resources are available to implement the processes.

Resources

In order to implement and manage doubleclick.net product described above, we will hire four additional senior software developers, as well as a system operations person, over the next two to six months.

Placement

The majority of doubleclick.net employees will be in sales and marketing.[21] We are selling to two customers: advertisers and websites. For advertisers, we envision selling direct initially, then through specialized reps who currently sell advertising to a specific vertical industry. Reps might include existing publishers, brokers, or direct-marketing organizations. We will use direct sales and telesales to focus on ad agencies and advertisers. Our focus for the first year will be on the affinity groups discussed earlier. Over time, we will organize the sales force along vertical industry lines.

We can sell the doubleclick.net service to large, existing ad-based websites. They typically already have advertisers, and this would be a quick way to produce revenue and to discourage these sites from becoming future competition.

We will use telemarketing to acquire websites. Becoming a member of doubleclick.net is completely automated, so we suspect many websites will become familiar with the service and subscribe directly through our website.

---

21 This sentence passed for the traditional "management" section in our business plan. Since there were only two of us at that point, we simply attached our résumés to the end of the plan.

However, you should include a brief section on management. When you do, remember, less is more. I wouldn't go very deeply into the background of your management team; offer a brief overview. People want to see executives with a track record of success, so stress track records. If you went to Harvard, that's great. If you went to Lansing Community College, don't stress it. Don't only mention what company you worked for; talk about the successes you had while you were there.

Promotion

A strong promotional campaign is key to our success. The Internet is hot, and everyone wants to talk about it, so we should be able to garner attention and interest. Public relations will play a large role in announcing our existence to the world. Initially, we will target advertising and direct-marketing publications such as *Ad Age*, *Adweek*, and *Direct Marketing*. We will also target computer publications to attract both advertisers and websites in the computer industry.

We will conduct "Target Advertising on the Internet" seminars for ad agencies. We will initially target San Francisco, Boston, and New York. While in these locations, we will also hold seminars for websites.

Of course, doubleclick.net advertising will be a primary marketing vehicle. We want the world of advertisers and websites to know about the power of doubleclick.net. We will purchase advertising space from a major website and develop highly targeted ads for the following industries:

- Advertising
- Computer
- Publication and media
- Websites
- Computer analysts
- Entertainment
- Travel

We will attend and speak at ad-agency, direct-marketing, and Web trade shows to promote doubleclick.net. In all of our promotional efforts, our goal is to direct the prospects to our website.

Pricing

Targeting brings enormous price savings for the advertiser. We price ads according to the number of target selection criteria. The price per ad increases with targeting; however, the cost of a target ad versus a "shotgun" (nontargeted) ad decreases substantially. It is in the advertiser's and double click.net's best interest to target ads. If we are efficient in selling highly targeted ads, we will be able to increase the revenue per ad far beyond two cents per ad. We will provide a 15 percent discount for all qualified ad agencies.

doubleclick.net benefits websites by reducing or even eliminating their sales and marketing overhead, as well as increasing their advertising impressions. We can help both small and large websites double their revenue.

Website Advertising Comparison	Pre-IAF	IAF
Average price per ad	0.02	0.031
Sales and advertising expense	25%	15%
Ad space sold	50%	100%
Gross profit per ad	0.0075	0.0130
Website gross profit increase		74%
Minimum revenue sharing percent to website	24%	

For the *ad space sold* percent, we assume based on experience that most advertising sites are nowhere near 100 percent advertising capacity. The *minimum revenue sharing percent to website* is the minimum revenue sharing percent we must give to be equivalent to the pre-doubleclick.net situation. In the above model, the revenue sharing split is 50 percent.

One alternative to revenue sharing is to simply buy bulk ads from websites. Based on Lycos pricing, we believe we can buy ads for less than 1.5 cents per ad. In the model above, we are paying about 1.43 cents per ad. If we are able to sell a greater percentage of highly targeted ads, we can substantially increase our profits through buying ads rather than through revenue sharing. However, through revenue sharing, we effectively minimize our risks of unsold ad space.

An interesting calculation is the minimum cost of delivering an ad at maximum system capacity. At 100 percent efficiency, an ad costs only an astounding .05 cents to deliver. Even with the system working at only 10 percent capacity, the cost of a single ad still costs .5 cents to deliver.

Competition[22]

As with any market, there is significant competition and potential competition. Of course, we are competing for advertising dollars in general; however, we will examine only the Internet advertising marketplace.

High-Traffic Websites

There are a number of existing high-traffic websites, like Lycos, Playboy, and Yahoo!, that already have advertisers. These sites each have the ability to place 10MM ads each month and probably can afford to sell to advertisers. In addition, advertisers who want to begin Internet advertising will most likely become aware of these sites and prefer to work with one large site rather than many small sites.

Lycos, the most popular search server on the Internet, has recently introduced an advertising program displaying ads that relate to the search request. For example, if a user searched for "laptop computers," a Toshiba ad might be displayed. This is a good mechanism for targeting advertising; however, you would need a very large inventory of ads to match the almost infinite combination of search requests.

Fortunately, these same sites are also potential customers for doubleclick.net, even if they keep their existing advertisers. High-traffic websites can use doubleclick.net to sell ad inventory. doubleclick.net will target these large sites and make attractive offers to join doubleclick.net. We suspect that none of these sites will be able to afford to replicate the doubleclick.net internet profiles database (IP-DB) used in ad matching.

Online Service Providers (OSPs)

OSPs such as AOL, Prodigy, MSN, and CompuServe already have relationships with many companies, content providers, and advertisers. OSPs can afford to create an IP-DB and combine this with their own membership profiles.

---

22 "Competitors" is a key section. You will see that we spend a lot of time on it. Not only do you have to address your direct competitors, but you also have to discuss the tangential competitors, companies that could come into your space. You can delude yourself into thinking major companies won't compete with you, but if you're successful, they will. Talk about them. Investors like to see paranoid executives.

The Internet strategy for the OSPs is unclear at the moment. It would appear that each is intent on becoming an internet service provider (ISP) as well as supporting content development. The OSPs could become our biggest marketing opportunity or our greatest competitor.

Publishers and Broadcasters Moving to the Internet

Many traditional publishers and broadcasters are moving their content to the Internet. *USA Today*, *The Wall Street Journal*, ESPN, and every television network have presences on the Internet. They already have strong existing relationships with their advertisers, to whom they can sell Internet ads.

Fortunately, these sites are also potential customers for doubleclick.net, even if they keep their existing advertisers. Publisher and broadcasting websites can use doubleclick.net to sell ad inventory. doubleclick.net will target these large sites and make attractive offers to join doubleclick.net. We suspect that none of these sites will be able to easily replicate the doubleclick.net internet profiles database (IP-DB) used in ad matching. Alternatively, we can sell the doubleclick.net service to these large existing ad-based websites. They typically already have advertisers, and this would be a quick way to produce revenue and discourage these sites from becoming future competition.

Subscription Services

Just like OSPs, there are a number of subscription services on the Internet. Typically, subscription services are free of advertising. Consequently, subscription sites cost money to join. Subscription services are a threat to the entire Internet advertising industry. Our belief is that advertising-based websites will far exceed subscription-based sites. Indeed, subscription-based sites could be candidates for doubleclick.net advertising.

Doubleclick.net Copycats

Even as you read this, there could be other doubleclick.net-like services on the horizon. Clearly, the advertising problem is an attractive one to solve. Focalink, Interactive Media, Katz, and Petry appear to be the most likely competitors.

To create a competitive system would most likely take at least six months. Even though the doubleclick.net service is seemingly simple, the back-end technology is quite complex. The creation and maintenance of the IP-DB are critical in performing accurate ad matchings. The algorithms involved with the scheduling and real-time ad matching are quite sophisticated. We will protect most of this back-end technology as a trade secret. As in any market, market share is the best defense to competition. If we are first and able to build a critical mass quickly, market leadership is ours to lose.

Following is a detailed feature comparison between various advertising alternatives:

Risks[23]

In this section, we identify the major risks to doubleclick.net. We rate each threat according to risk and probability of occurrence.

Competition

Even though the implementation of doubleclick.net will be considerable, others can replicate our work in as little as six to twelve months. We currently do not believe the product is patentable, thus we are relying on trade secrets to keep the barriers a bit higher.

As discussed in the pricing section, the cost to deliver an ad at maximum efficiency is only .02 cents per ad. This could force the Internet ads to become a commodity if supply far outstrips demand.

Risk: medium
Probability: high

---

23 You don't want to surprise anyone. That's why you talk about the big risks. Specifically, you want to talk about: where they could happen; what the probability is of their happening; and what you will do if they happen. You want to show potential investors that you have taken all this into account; you also want to show them how you think. Investors look at entrepreneurs who do this and say, "You know what? This idea may not work, but these people are smart enough to figure out a new strategy if they have to."

	Weight	Newspapers	Magazines	Cable TV	Direct Mail	Internet Ads	IAN
Ability to control frequency	1	3	2	3	2	3	1
Ability to control reach	1	2	2	2	1	3	1
Ability to test market	1	2	3	3	1	2	1
Ability to track purchase	1	2	3	3	1	3	2
Depth of information	1	3	3	2	2	1	1
Geographic flexibility	1	1	3	2	1	3	1
National coverage cost	1	3	1	1	3	1	1
Opportunity for exposure	1	3	3	2	3	1	1
Personalization	1	3	2	2	2	3	1
Regional cost	1	1	2	3	2	3	1
Response tracking	1	2	3	3	1	3	1
Sense of immediacy	1	2	3	2	1	1	1
Targeting or concentration	1	3	2	2	1	2	1
Controlled circulation	2	3	1	3	2	3	1
Delivery control	2	1	3	1	3	3	1
Ease of placing ad	2	2	2	3	3	2	1
High fidelity color	2	3	1	1	1	2	2
Mass market	2	2	1	1	3	3	3
Production costs	2	2	2	3	3	1	1
Sight and sound	2	3	3	1	3	3	3
Catalog value	3	3	1	3	3	1	1
Closing date flexibility	3	2	3	3	2	3	1
Ethnic appeal	3	1	1	2	1	3	3
Pass-along audience	3	3	1	3	3	3	3
User control	3	2	2	3	2	1	1
Vehicle life	3	2	1	3	3	1	1

Selectivity/targeting criterion

	Weight	Newspapers	Magazines	Cable TV	Direct Mail	Internet Ads	IAN
Area of interest	1	3	1	3	1	3	1
Company primary SIC	1	3	2	3	1	3	1
Company revenue	1	3	3	3	1	3	1
Company secondary SIC	1	3	2	3	1	3	1
Frequency	1	3	2	2	1	3	1
Geographic location	1	1	3	1	1	3	1
Job function/title	1	3	1	3	1	3	1
Operating system	1	3	1	3	1	3	1
Reach	1	3	2	3	1	3	1
Type of organization (eg. edu, mil)	1	3	2	3	1	3	1
User interests	1	2	1	2	1	2	1
Website demographics	1	3	3	3	3	2	1
Website(s)	1	3	3	3	3	1	1
Date and time	2	1	3	2	2	3	1
Likelihood to respond	2	3	3	3	2	3	1
Ads already viewed	2	3	3	3	3	3	1
Company # of employees	3	3	3	3	1	3	1
Company name	3	3	3	3	1	3	1
Date	3	1	3	1	2	3	1
Gender	3	3	1	1	1	3	1
Internet/online Service Provider	3	3	3	3	2	3	1
Throughput	3	3	3	3	3	3	1
Web browser	3	3	3	3	3	3	1

Ratings: 1 = excellent 2 = good 3 = poor

Internet Ads Go Bust

Internet advertising is new and unproven. However, we believe the market is viable. The ability to target and measure who sees an ad is just too compelling.

Risk: high
Probability: low

Ad Filter

Somebody could create either a Web browser or a Web browser add-on to filter out all advertising. I doubt the major Web browser manufacturers would do such a thing, since they typically also make Web server software that ad-based websites buy. A more likely scenario would be for somebody to write a winsock DLL that sits between any Web browser and TCP/IP stack. This DLL would simply filter out HTTP requests to all services like doubleclick.net.

It is important that ads do not become annoying to users, or they would be willing to insert such a filter on their PC. In any case, only a small percentage of people would ever run such a filter.

There are two ways to defeat such an add-on. The first would be to correlate a website log with our own ad log for the site. We could detect users not requesting ads and prohibit them from future website access. Another method, which requires testing, is to secure all ad pages (using SSL technology now common in Web browsers and servers) so the filter would be unable to tamper with the encrypted page.

Risk: low
Probability: high

Caching

Some OSPs, proxy servers, and Web browsers cache Web pages to reduce traffic demands and speed access. Caching stores a Web page locally so when either the same user or another user (in the case of an OSP or proxy server) accesses the same page, it is retrieved locally rather than over the network again. What started as a kind gesture toward the Net presents a bit of a problem for impression-based advertising, since a single impression might be viewed by many users.

There are three solutions to this problem. We can "expire" a Web page to force the cache to reload it on subsequent accesses. We do not know currently how many OSPs and proxy servers will honor this command. We will discover during development how effective the expire command is with proxy servers.

The second solution involves getting "hit" rates from the OSPs. As doubleclick.net represents a large number of websites, we need to take the leadership role in obtaining this information. The OSPs will most likely favor working with a single organization rather than potentially thousands of individual websites. Proxy servers should not be a major issue (today, at least) because firewalls are more common in organizations, and most proxy servers honor HTTP expire and no-cache headers.

The third solution brings into question the legality of caching systems. Is caching legal? Probably not, because caching a copyrighted page deprives the owner of economic value.

Risk: low
Probability: medium

Privacy

Today users can access a Web server anonymously, and they know it. With doubleclick.net, a user is not so anonymous. Even though doubleclick.net may not know who the user is by name, the user could become unsettled when an ad follows him around or seems to know she is running a UNIX system in San Francisco for a paper manufacturer. It will be feasible over time to definitively track a large percentage of individuals and learn their likes and dislikes.

In order to minimize the privacy issue, doubleclick.net will keep all user information confidential. Advertisers and websites will have access only to anonymous profile information. We will make sure users are aware of this.

Risk: low
Probability: medium

Future

Fortunately, there is substantial additional functionality we can add to doubleclick.net, as well as additional markets where we can expand with doubleclick.net. This section briefly describes some potential double-click.net futures.

Directory Service

Create an e-mail company mailing list and Net-news directory service based on the information collected for doubleclick.net. We would have by far the most comprehensive directory service, which we could use for both advertising and information collecting from subscribers.

Ad Targeting Service

Allow websites to offer targeting for their advertisers. This would minimize the threat of large websites developing their own targeting system. Many large sites (like ESPN) will want account control but will need targeting to compete with doubleclick.net. In addition, this would create an effective distribution channel for doubleclick.net.

Coupons

We can create electronic coupons that would encourage the user to buy but would also more accurately track the relationship between advertising and a purchase.

Self-Advertising Websites

A large number of very active websites are owned by companies that use the Web to complement existing forms of communications, like telephone, mail, and BBS systems. The Internet offers an inexpensive means for delivering information and customer services. We believe these organizations, which might already be advertisers with doubleclick.net, could benefit from doubleclick.net by advertising *their own* products to users who access *their* site. For example, when a user running Windows 3.1 accesses the Microsoft site, perhaps a Windows 95 ad could be displayed.

We can sell this same service to Web shopping sites. When a prospect enters the server, doubleclick.net can tell her about the special they are running that matches her profiles. This is a very powerful service for the website.

International Company Profiles

Our initial focus is on the U.S., though in the future, we will obtain similar profiles on non-U.S. companies.

User Surveys

Sponsor contests encouraging users to fill out profiles about themselves. Of course, we will target only users whom we can uniquely identify but we're lacking information about.

Consumer Demographics

Once we identify a user and have information such as telephone number and/or address, we can obtain detailed demographic information from any number of consumer research groups.

Universal Bingo Card

We can offer advertisers a universal bingo card for sending users additional information. Once we have the information, users would no longer need to fill out a bingo card when requesting information. We can charge a small fee for the lead, as well as continue to build our IP-DB.

Variations of Ads

An advertiser can produce a number of similar ads that could be linked to specific information such as country or throughput. So, for example, Coke could display Japanese ads from all users originating from Japan, or animated ads for all users attached to the Internet on a high-speed network.

Multiple Ad Placements

We will want to offer various types of ads (placement and size) at different prices. For example, a top-banner ad would be more expensive than a bottom-banner ad.

Fraud Detector

Eventually, some website will create a program to connect to their site and inflate their advertising revenue. We will be able to detect this type of fraud fairly easily by examining doubleclick.net log files.

Fault Tolerance

We will need the system to be available 24x7x365 with minimal downtime. We will have a hot backup of the system, though there are other measures we can take to ensure fault tolerance.

International Expansion

There is no reason we can't establish doubleclick.net servers and sales offices in countries around the world. In fact, there is no reason, other than efficiency, why the current doubleclick.net system cannot process international ads.

doubleclick.net Direct

Provide a turnkey direct-order service over the Internet. When a user clicks the ad, he is displayed additional information and is able to place the order directly over the Internet. doubleclick.net would receive advertising as well as revenue for every transaction.

Site Profile Analysis

We can perform detailed profile analysis for commercial websites in batch or real time. There are several site-auditing packages currently on the market; however, none appears to have the level of profile detail that doubleclick.net does.

Auto Target

An advertiser starts with a nontargeted ad campaign, and doubleclick.net learns which users are most likely to take an ad jump. As doubleclick.net learns, the ads become more targeted on a likely target.[24]

---

24 This covers the basics. Everything else you might include isn't that interesting. You can have a list of people with impressive credentials who are on the board. If you want, you can include a few well-selected references and collateral material. But to me, that isn't as important as telling people what you are going to do and why you are going to succeed. I would focus more on simplicity than on completeness. Weight doesn't win.

ACKNOWLEDGMENTS

I can't imagine who reads this section, but here goes. I want to thank all those who helped me throughout the years in my various ventures.

First, Joan and Al (my parents), who always encouraged my experiments, even when they put our house in jeopardy.

I was fortunate to have a bunch of great teachers and coaches at Detroit Catholic Central. I never got to thank Frank Garlicki before he died, but Frank, you always told us to think big, and I tried. At the University of Michigan, I was taught by some of the greatest professors. I still feel bad that I turned down the U of M Ph.D. program to pursue my first startup, ICC. Thanks, Professor Haddad, for going to bat for me.

I am always grateful that all my brothers and sisters (Michael, David, Karen, and Kathy) encouraged me to end school and pursue the startup. Maybe you saw something in me that I hadn't seen.

I learned a lot with my first partners at ICC: Bill Miller, Mike Schier, Larry Duckworth, Ralph McIntyre, and Pete Miller. We had a crazy and great time building that company.

I still think that my best management training came from being an assistant wrestling coach at Cincinnati Moeller. Jeff Gaier, the head coach, is a great inspiration to me. I learned that if you can get a group of boys/men to do anything, it's easy to get professionals to do a great job!

I especially want to thank Frank Pritt for effectively firing me from my job at Attachmate.

I was lucky to meet Chris Klaus of ISS back in 1995. Chris was so much like me when I was young, but he listened better and learned more quickly. You and Tom Noonan have built a brilliant, successful company, and I was fortunate to play a small part in ISS's success.

Much of DoubleClick's success is directly attributable to Dwight Merriman and Kevin Ryan. When I was young, I always considered myself to be a great engineer, until I met Dwight. Dwight doesn't know what "it can't be done" means. He always finds a way. I was blessed to have Kevin Ryan take over from me as CEO of DoubleClick. Kevin took over right when some of the country's most difficult economic times hit. Today, DoubleClick remains a very strong and healthy company.

Dave Strohm is a true venture capitalist. If only some day I could be half as wise as you. I'll always be indebted to you for all your help.

There are, of course, countless others who helped me along the way. The thousands of employees who shared the same visions and worked hard to bring the visions to life—thank you.

I'd like to thank Rafe Sagalyn, my agent, and John Mahaney, my publisher. Thank you to those in production: Susan Westendorf, John Sharp, Lenny Henderson, and David Tran. Thanks, Pat Garner, for your early suggestions. And Paul Brown, my cowriter and book writing spiritual guide who helped me through this process and hopefully made me sound more profound than I actually am.

INDEX

ABOUT THE AUTHOR

Kevin O'Connor is chairman of DoubleClick and on the board of many other public and private companies. He has several other ventures in the planning stages and is a private investor helping to fund the next wave of technology companies. He lives in Santa Barbara, California, with his wife Nancy and their three kids.